IN SILENCE THEY RETURN

A Message of Spiritual Assurance

BY JUDY BOSS

1972
LLEWELLYN PUBLICATIONS
Saint Paul, Minnesota 55165, USA

ISBN-0-87542-080-X
First printing 1972

Publisher: LLEWELLYN PUBLICATIONS, St. Paul, Minnesota
Typographer: Chester-Kent, Inc., St. Paul, Minnesota
Lithographer: R. R. Donnelley and Sons Co., Chicago, Illinois

Printed in the United States of America

To Phyllis, Marilyn and the many others here who have made this possible; and to those that have gone beyond——I humbly thank you.

Introduction

"Death is not really the end," I said to my neighbor shortly after my husband was killed, leaving me with five small children to raise alone. "For him, it is an exciting new adventure." And for me life is a challenge that I have to face. I have no time for tears."

However, my days ached with the exhaustion of my responsibilities and the nights were long and lonely until one day an insurance man came to my door and happened to mention a woman he had known that did automatic writing—a form of communication with the dead. "I could do that," I said. "I know I can." After trying for a few days I began to communicate in writing with my dead husband, my mother and father and later, many other spirits. My life began to acquire a new dimension of knowledge and interest for myself and others.

"How do you do it?" I am asked so often. I pray and then in silence I sit with pen held over paper until my hand seems to move like it was mechanical and separate from the rest of my body. It starts slowly but moves faster and faster while lines appear on the paper. Sometimes circles, symbols or perhaps a name appears. This is their introduction. Then I begin to hear, back into the recesses of my mind, someone speaking to me and I record what I hear. Sometimes I don't hear very well and then my hand becomes very mechanical again and tries to scratch it out in shaky circular writing. Often I am referred to a book or a map to clarify things for me. The messages I receive may be directed to those who have asked for them or may speak in general philosophy of life or the after life, but they are always meaningful and it consistently amazes me how accurate they are at perceiving straight to the center of a problem.

"How can I believe you? Tell me something so that I can really believe this is true." The intent, serious voice that pleaded with me one evening was that of a world famous symphony conductor. "Perhaps I can't convince you." I said. "But that does not really matter for instead I hope to open a new door for you to investigate and explore so that you can find your own meaning—your own belief."

I remain sceptical. I call myself an "open sceptic" for I want to keep my intellect always open for new growth but whenever I become too doubtful something always happens to make me realize that there seems to be more evidence to believe than to not believe.

The Long Lonely Night

"Damn him! damn him! damn him!" I exploded, as I rolled over in bed and looked at the clock for the tenth time that night.

"5:30 in the morning! Where is he?" I raged to myself.

After thirteen years of living with my high-spirited Irishman, I knew well what it was like to wait for him to come home. There always seemed to be one more stop at one more bar for one last beer. Eating cold dinners with the children and sitting alone at night, worrying and waiting, was not a new experience for me, but this was too much! Out all night was too much! I'd like to take his head and knock it against a wall. He's out playing, and I'm home chewing my fingernails. It just wasn't fair.

"Damn him!" I sputtered again.

I got up and straightened the bed. The sheets had become rumpled and twisted as I had tossed and turned for hours. Fleeting pictures flashed through my mind. Was he in a ditch somewhere? Was he with another woman? Where was he? Why didn't he call? I tried to comfort myself with the thought that if he were in an accident, someone would call me. It didn't work. What if he needed help somewhere?

"Damn him, why doesn't he call?" The stillness of the night was broken only by my mutterings and by an occasional snore or cough from sleeping children. My blessings, I thought with unabashed pride; five beautiful, healthy, intelligent, happy children. I walked through the house and looked at them.

The girls' room was filled with hair ribbons, dolls, stuffed animals and pink things. Joyful, giggly, pretty Kathleen lay quiet now, her arms mothering protectively around her little white poodle, resting for another fun filled day with her many friends. Across the room, with long blond hair haloing gently around her sweet face, slept bouncy and bubbly six year old Mary. Was she dreaming of becoming a ballerina, I wondered. How she loved to dance—pirouetting and spinning around the living room floor.

Downstairs, the boys' room held a different scene—dirty sox and underwear, model airplanes and ski posters. Competitive and intense, Kevin lay now in exhausted sleep. On the wall behind him hung rows of shiny gold and silver ski medals, proof of hard work and an abundance of natural ability. He looked peaceful now, his humorous, teasing smile gone. As I watched, his body seemed to grow before my eyes, so eager was he to become a teenager and face more challenges in life. His opposite was pensive, easy going Mike. Four years younger than Kevin, he was a kind and sensitive dreamer. Behind the freckles of his loveable face was a ray of gentle sunshine. Now, in his baseball pajamas he slept as a child but tomorrow, maybe in many tomorrow's he would become a philosopher or poet.

Such an exciting assortment of personalities I thought as I walked into the last bedroom. Jimmy's three year old chubby little body lay disheveled on the large bed. His gorgeous blue eyes were closed. The voluptuous laughter that brought tears of joy to my eyes was silent now. Sharing his love and curiosity for life brought me so much happiness! Unable to resist his charm, I kissed him softly on his cheek and tiptoed out of his room.

I opened the draperies in the living room and looked out at the rolling hills of the Minnesota countryside. The towering trees and the gentle pond usually gave me a feeling of serenity, but not now. As if searching for my relief, my mind drifted back to a happier time—a day when we had taken the children skiing.

It was warm and the bright sun softened the snow and tanned our faces—just right for a lunch outdoors. Mary and Jimmy played in the snow around me, as I laid out the food on the picnic table and then began scanning the area for Mac.

My eyes caught sight of him—down the hill he came, flying with the wind behind him and the snow blowing in

his face. Dressed in navy, his dark body staccatoed against
the silvery snow. He looked like a pendulum swinging and
swaying back and forty; so smooth and easy. The world
and he seemed in such perfect attunement. He was in
command of himself! He was free!

"Hey dad!" Kevin yelled at the bottom. "I almost
beat you."

"You're really skiing fast Kev, and you too, Mike."
He answered.

"Ahh dad," Mike returned disgruntledly, "I fall all
the time."

"I know," Kathleen added, "You fell right in front of
me. I almost bombed into you!"

I watched Mac as he wiped the snow from his boots.
It didn't matter whether he was adjusting his skis, baiting a
fish line or sailing a boat; he became more alive and vital in
the freedom of the outdoors. His skin was weathered and
coppery from many hours in the sun. Small wrinkles
laughed around his lips while the firm lines of his nose gave
strength to the handsome face that topped the strong,
stocky body. His craggy eyebrows and thick curly hair
gleamed with touches of silver. As he lit up his pipe he
provided the final embellishment to his masculine image.
But it was the eyes—the gleam and twinkle in those
scampering blue eyes, that really gave him away and
became the clue to the mischief and merriment of my
fun-loving Irishman.

"Michael me boy, how about getting me my guitar?"
he said in his fake Irish brogue.

"Ahh dad," The kids groaned.

"You don't even know how to play it," Mary added.

"Well, I'm learning. What I need now is a little wine, a little music, and a little rest," he said as he stretched out on the snow.

The guitar began to plink, plink, plunk . . .

The vision dissolved as I saw the small white sports car roll up the driveway. Mac stopped the car and as he got out, he saw me through the living room window. A weak look of concern passed over his face and then was gone. As he walked up the front steps his shoulders sagged and his footsteps were slow and heavy. Carrying his coat, with his tie off, shirt unbuttoned and suit rumpled, he looked defeated.

He walked into the room and I saw that he was sober. My anger gave way to worry about him. The sleepless night of anxiety left me weak and defenseless. I sighed deeply and waited for him to speak.

Slumping into the chair next to me he said, "I know, I know I should have called. I'm sorry."

It was like a broken record that I had heard so many times before. I had no reply and started to walk out of the room.

"No, wait, please I want to tell you something." He said.

"I've been with Tim Sullivan tonight. I haven't seen him since college, and has he changed! He's been living in the ghetto and working with the people there. Judy, you have no idea how desperate and poor those people are."

As he talked, a look of such infinite sadness crossed

his face and then gave way to a piercing hurt of frustration. It compelled me to look away.

"Their needs are so great," he went on, getting angry. "It's almost impossible for us to understand how people can live under such subhuman conditions. They have food stamps, but still they know what hunger is. Meanwhile, here's middle class America fighting the obesity problem. It doesn't make sense!"

"But," I protested, "can't they work, can't they find jobs somewhere?"

"Don't you understand?" he yelled, becoming impatient, they're the losers, they're the losers of the God Damn richest country in the world. They're the cripples—in mind and spirit. They just don't have the know-how, the guts, the smarts to pull themselves out of the pits they're in. They need help! They've been knocked around for generations. They sleep and eat with rats, and that's what they think of themselves—just another rat! What a self-image!"

"But, but," I said, "They're not all like that . . ."

"Listen," he interrupted, "Tim had someone with him, John, John Redhorse. John's wife is expecting their fourth baby and he doesn't have a job. No one wants to hire him. He's not trained, and he's an Indian. He lives with his father and uncle—eight of them in three rooms. I took him home. Shit! it's no bigger than an outhouse—windows covered up with tar paper—that's home?"

"What about all of the government agencies?" I argued. "I've read about so many new projects to help."

"Tokenism," he interrupted again, "that's all it is. A lot of understaffed, underpaid, and overworked people all bottled up in red tape. Now the God Damn government wants to pull the group Tim works for. Tim's been doing some great things but it looks like the funding is going to be cut off. America is more interested in sending people to the moon than solving their problems here.

"Judy, I'd like to quit my job and go help those people. I'd just like to show them someone cares. They're human beings–Damn it! I've got to do something for them."

His eyes were watery and glazed and as the tears dripped down his face he seemed to stare right through me, as if I were made of tissue paper.

What about us? I thought, who will feed us?

Thump! "Mommy, mommy!" Jimmy had fallen from his bed. Awakened by the screams, five hungry little bodies scrambled into the kitchen, where they began pulling cereal boxes down from the shelves. Another day had begun.

Mac got up, showered, shaved and went to work.

A Tired American

The long lonely nights became more frequent as Mac thrashed back and forth in his mind what to do. He was torn by anxiety to help a troubled world but at the same time bound by love and obligations to his family. As his restlessness increased he seemed to find fault in every area of life. The problems of humanity consumed him and his conscience compelled him to do something. "What can I do?" he would say. How he could help this society that needed help so badly was a nightmare that he couldn't escape. It preyed on him day and night. Gradually he gave up the idea of working in the ghetto. True, the needs there were ever more pressing, but so were our children's. There had to be another way. But finding that way was difficult.

"If it weren't for the buck—that insidious buck!" Mac grumbled one morning as he was shaving.

"Money is a fact of life," I reminded him. "We can't live without it."

"Hell!", he yelled over the drone of the electric razor, "its more than that. Money has become an obsession with people. Buy, buy buy, our TV sets scream at us. Buy this, buy that! Our kids are weaned on it. Why, we are p opigating a society of sophisticated materialists. The answer to America's dream is the buck—our mixed-up society strives for the dollar! And what does it give them but the desire for more. It becomes an unquenchable thirst, dries up their souls and leaves them panting for more. More! More!" he yelled.

"Hey cool it," I said, "not everybody . . . ."

"Look!" he yelled, "Don't tell me, I know. I'm a stock broker, you know. I see it every day. Everybody wants money, money, money. What do you think I hear all day long? My music is phones ringing, ringing, ringing; a crazy rhythm that pounds in my ear—Is the market going up? I'm asked. Should I buy? Is the market going down? Should I sell? Up—down, down—up. What do they think I am, some God damn prophet? Up—down, down—up!" he yelled. "It's like a fucking merry-go-round!"

I recoiled from the sound of the obscenity and started toward the door, but he grabbed my arm—"You can call it whatever you want but that's what it is. It's a fucking merry-go-round!" he shouted. "Round and round it goes with everyone churning, groping, stretching until their guts explode and their souls reel with turmoil, just so they can grab that beautiful golden ring—The Almighty Buck!"

"Get out of it," I yelled. "Get out of that job!"

"Fine! Great!" he said in exasperation. "What am I going to do? I've been a broker for nine years. What else could I do? I'm not trained for anything else. Don't you see," he said pleadingly, "I'm trapped! I'm in a corner of a big black box and can't get out!"

"Look," I said, "I can work. I've been thinking it over; in fact, I've called the University. I just need a few more credits for my teacher's certificate. I could teach while you find something else."

"No, No, you've got enough with five kids," he answered. "That's not right."

"Then what is?" I asked.

"I don't know right now. I just don't know."

He went to work.

But, he left me with his aura of dissatisfaction. He can't seem to fit anything good in the world, I mumbled to myself as I cleaned up the breakfast dishes. All he sees are the problems, the ugly and the inhuman. Every few months it seemed to be something else that griped his emotions like a vice and left him angry and frustrated. Next it was the war that received the vent of his wrath.

"Judy, I'm so God damn sick of this war. Vietnam, Cambodia, Laos—it just goes on and on. The omnipotent United States thinks it can solve all of the world's problems when it can't even solve its own. War seems to be the answer to war as the vicious killing machine creeps into country after country. I met a priest today that is doing something about the war. I've invited him over to our house to talk."

"What's it all about?" I asked.

"He is among a group of fourteen priests and ministers that are burning draft cards in protest to the war."

"But, what's that going to solve?" I asked.

"Well, besides boggling up the records they are laying their lives on the line for a cause they believe in. It'll show that lives are more important than draft cards. Americans have gotten so used to thousands dying in the war that they think nothing of it. Yet they get all excited about burning draft cards! Our sense of human values have been anesthetized. It's a sick society that regards a felony as more important than a murder. Do you think there would have been a Hitler if the Germans would have stood up in protest like these men are doing? Oh, Judy, I'd like to do the same thing."

"But, I protest," I said. "You'll end up in jail." "They will too, you know, those fourteen men," he answered. "I know, I know what you are going to say: They don't have five children."

Two nights later he read me a poem he had written.
Fourteen people standing all about
standing, crying, burning
records, records, records, up in smoke

Freedom is the message that its all about
Freedom from the machine that tries to
eat us all

Fourteen men laying down their life
for the rest of humanity
for you—for me

Burglary, arson! all the people shout
Freedom, freedom comes the answer back

Who hears it?
One says the goal is good
Others say the methods are wrong
Very few can listen

People seem important
that we all agree
Paper! Paper! has to be secondary

Burn paper, burn
Freedom is the message!

There were tears in both of our eyes as he finished.
"What can I do?" he said in despair. "I've got to do
something," he said. "I've got to." I couldn't tell him no,
because I felt these men were doing a courageous thing.
But for Mac? no, I didn't want Mac to go to jail. I was
selfish and wanted him home with our family but I felt
guilty so I kept silent. As I cried myself to sleep that night

I begged God to find another way for Mac.
I was very worried. I loved him. I admired his ideals
and believed in his cause, but I was disturbed by the
change in him. He was so frantic. He seemed in a frenzied
mood of excitement all the time. He was either very up or
very down. He could not sit and relax with me or the
children anymore. In fact, he could not sit still at all. How
could he keep this up? I wondered. His problems were so
great and so deep that I could not share mine with him. I
was lonely too, shut off by a wall of misery.

I gazed into his eyes and wondered if they would ever
be warm and tranquil again. His facial muscles had become
taut and tense. His voice was coarse and rough. His
language was threatening.

"You are capable of so much," I told him one night.
Yet, how could he—one man—do all he wanted to do?

I watched and wondered, waited and wept. Hoping he
could find his way, somehow, somewhere.

As the weeks passed, seeds of discontent had begun to
grow within him concerning the church that he had turned
to for strength and answers for over thirty years. Born and
raised in its heritage and culture he had depended on it for
security and adhered strongly to its tenets. But now as he
began to examine his own values he also questioned the
source of his religious training. How Christ's church could
preach brotherhood but not take a critical stand or assume
a dominant role in society as a moral guide on critical
issues disturbed him. The contradiction of its teaching but
not becoming involved itself, left him to doubt its worth.

"What is a church for?" He complained one Sunday as we drove home from Mass.

"Well," I answered, "I guess we really have to go back to the teachings of Christ for the answer."

"Right!" he boomed, "and didn't He say we were all one under God?"

"And people's color doesn't make any difference," Mike added.

"But how come there aren't any black people in our church, dad?" Mary asked.

"That's the problem, Mary," he answered. "There are too many churches that are afraid to handle the real gut level issues of our time. Integration is just too contraversial. People are afraid of it."

"It seems as if so much of church time is taken handling doctrines and problems within its own structure." I commented.

"Hell, they got time. It's how you use something that counts." Mac said. "Take money for example. I handle church money often. I see it invested in stocks and bonds, property and business, so it can grow to more and more money. People would be amazed to know where the money they give goes—more buiildings—more brick and mortar. What about the poor? What do they get? Well, we give them some turkeys for Christmas and then we'll have a clothing drive. That will hold them off for awhile."

"No, Mac—that's not always true and you know it." I argued.

"Look Judy, don't be naive. The church has become a fantastically powerful institution controlling great wealth."

"I wonder if Christ would like his church today?" Kevin asked.

"They wouldn't even let Him in, Kev," Mac said. "I can see it now. Dear loving, merciful Jesus Christ—is this your church? Come, come walk through the doors with me and see if this is your home. What? They won't let you in? Oh, I see, you are dirty. So dirty that you look black. There are no blacks in this neighborhood. We wouldn't want anyone else to be uncomfortable in your presence. Besides, your hair is long. You look messy, not nice and clean like the rest of us. Try somewhere else Christ. What? You have tried other places. Well, sorry about that, but we can't take you now. We have a building campaign coming up and we don't want people to be upset."

Where is Christianity, I thought as we drove the rest of the way home, but in the hearts and souls of man. People who want to give and love and sacrifice and die for it. Christianity is in you my troubled husband—in you who speaks and cries out for peace, love and equality for all men. I said a silent prayer that Christ would help Mac find His path.

We returned home from church and had breakfast. Mac was quiet and pensive as he ate. The children's jabber and silly chatter could not draw him out. Finally he got up and went to our bedroom and closed the door. I cleaned up the kitchen and then sat down to read the Sunday paper when he came to me with a worried look on his face and said he was going for a walk. Later, I went into the bedroom and saw some crumpled up paper on his desk. I was about to throw them away when I decided to open

them up and saw that he had been writing again. He titled
it WHERE ARE YOU JESUS? I read it slowly.

> Churches standing all around
> People all alone
> Churches everywhere
> People all alone
>
> All white
> All nice
> Never any words
> To make one want to think
>
> Churches all now empty
> Pews all a dusty
>
> Churches standing all around
> People free
> Churches everywhere
> People free
>
> Jesus, Jesus I love you
> Are you front and center
> In the middle of the pews?
>
> Or——are you in the back
> On the ground
> In the air
> Everywhere

I knew now that the comforts of the church were gone to him. He had opened its inner sanctuarys, searched deep inside its bowels, and found it cold and irrelevant to the goals he held. The institutions of society that he supported in youth, he now turned away from in anger. His church, his country, he no longer saw through idealistic eyes. As he gnawed away at their inequities his heart ached, and he bled both from them and for them.

Waking late one morning with Mac snoring next to me in heavy, deep sleep, I thought about his restlessness during the night. As he paced back and forth in the bedroom I drifted in and out of a troubled sleep. When I asked him what was wrong he responded quite sharply with, "Nothing—go back to sleep." But now it was morning and I could see by the strewn papers on his desk he had been writing most of the night. I picked up a sheet and read:

I AM A TIRED AMERICAN
I am tired of churches who preach equality
but cater to the moneyed class

I am tired of a government which continues
to destroy both people and land in Vietnam
for the name of freedom

I am a tired American . . . who feels a
Vietnam mother suffers pain as any other
person upon the death of a husband or
baby

I am a tired American . . . Tired of the
older generation who, in the name of
justice, refuses to let a black man
join "their club"

I am a tired American. Tired of nice
little Christians who refuse to let a
black man move into their neighborhood

I am a tired American who questions a
merciful Lord—why was he born an
American citizen, a nation under God,
with mercy and justice for all . . .
as long as you are white?

How long can he keep going like this? I thought as I
put the paper down. How can he keep tearing everthing
apart? I looked and I saw the suffering of a man who
wanted to turn the world upside down, shake it around,
and return it perfect. But he couldn't.

Then gradually, painfully through his turmoil he
seemed to come to a compromise with himself. Slowly he
began to understand more clearly his role in the big game
of life was to use the best resource he had—his voice. By
talking to people he hoped to catalyze their conscience
into action. And talk he did.

"You know," he said, "if I can only get people to
stop and think. If I can just wake up their sensitivities."

"Well, the way you shout and swear."

"I've got to," he interrupted, "Don't you realize? I

have to come on strong. That's the only way people will listen. They won't hear you if you nice-guy them along. I've got to go way out—to the extreme, maybe that will pull them off from dead center. Most people have tight little shells around them so they don't have to think—but, damn it! People have to think! They have to start thinking about others! All they think about is their own little world—their house—their car—their job. People are so damn selfish."

"You're right, and I do agree that talking is your thing. You're a salesman, and you sell your ideas to people every day."

"Right! I have to do things in the only way I can with people I know and work with. I've got to help people to realize they're human beings, not puppets, and it is they who are responsible for the society in which we live."

And so, talk he did. Everywhere he went it became a challenge; at the office, parties, meetings, bars. Wherever there were people he would talk. It was a consuming force inside him that never stopped. It drove him to great heights of joy and then frantic depths of despair. My gentle, loveable Teddy Bear, as I used to call him, became an angry lion.

People heard him. They listened and they began to think. There were those whose consciences had been awakened who felt the pangs of an injustice as he did. With them he felt hope. But then, there were others who turned him off. It was cozy and warm where they were; the outside could be threatening, so they pushed him away.

With them, he felt loneliness and dejection.

His depression was becoming a very real thing. He knew it and it scared him. Like the devil it chased and haunted him, sneaking up behind him when he least expected it. And so he ran. He escaped with every play mechanism he knew: skiing, drinking, partying. Day and night rolled into one. It amazed me how he could get by with so little sleep. He would ski all day Saturday and Sunday—the first one on the hill and the last to leave. Then he would stay up until two or three o'clock each night.

"How can he do it?" I asked myself. There seemed to be no stopping him or slowing him down, and I finally gave up trying. Like the drummer, he had to march to his own beat. I could only wait and watch and worry.

One evening we went to a church dinner and heard a speaker discuss problems within the church. The atmosphere was heavy with dissatisfaction and frustration. Priests were questioning their roles and lay people were asking "What can I do?"

Mac was in his element, while sipping brandy he argued and challenged those around him. The evening became long and late. I grew tired of hearing the same arguments that I had heard so many times before. Most people had left hours before I finally persuaded Mac to go downstairs and get our coats. The janitor was sweeping the floor. Most of the lights had been turned off and the hall was dark and still as the echoes of many voices had stopped. Wearily, I sat on the steps with my coat on as I waited for him to finish a few more verbal exchanges with a young priest. He said goodbye, then slowly walked toward me. His voice was soft and sad and as he looked deep into my eyes he said, "Judy, you're not going to understand this, but someday I'm going to leave you. It's not because I don't love you and the children, but because I have something important to do."

Icy chills shot up and down my body while angry, confused emotions passed through me. Understand? He was right! Oh dear God, what now?

The Labyrinth of Life

"Look, it just doesn't make any sense, that's all," Mac argued with me one evening. "If the world is supposed to be making progress—if it's getting any better, why in the hell are we still killing each other?"

"But Mac," I said impatiently, "the world evolves. Our evolutionary cycles go up and down. But we still improve. We progress. Sure we still have lots of problems—"

"Problems! Hell!" he yelled, "We haven't solved the most important. Man is just as immoral now as when time began. How does your conscience explain napalming innocent people in Viet Nam?"

"It's not right. I agree. But I still feel that the world is a better place to live than when man began."

"It is not. And will not be," he screamed, "until man

can live in peace. Don't you see? All of these thousands of years and we are still just as bad off? What's the use? What's the God Damn reason for life if we're not able to make it any better? And who cares? We just go on and on making the same mistakes. What the hell, it's hopeless!"

"No! No!" I argued. "It's not hopeless. As long as there are people, there is hope. You're too impatient. You just can't see the progress because it's slow. One lifetime is too short a period—"

"Hell!" he interrupted, "That's all I've got is one life so what does it matter, you know? I can't change it. If man wants to destroy himself I can't prevent him."

"Don't you have any faith in God?" I asked.

There was silence. He thought for awhile and then said, "Faith? Yes, I have faith in people. I love people. But God? I don't know. I just don't know. Life just doesn't have any meaning. It just doesn't make sense."

He would give up for awhile. Then with a jolt start over again with a new idea and fresh outlook. Like an alternating current he would charge back and forth with deep bursts of energy from despair to hope. His life style had become a dichotomy with his humanistic ideals at odds with his materialistic business life. There were intervals for him—not of peace, but of a frantic search for fun. He loved being with people. Laughing, drinking, singing with his friends brought the joy he desperately needed. Fun became the safety valve for the boiling pressure inside him. But I could not share his laughter. I worried about the frenzied, almost hungry way he was devouring life. The evenings out would always be long; he hated to have them end.

"Life is so difficult for Mac," I complained to my good friend Mary one day. "He is so disturbed with himself and everyone around him. I know he's got problems and his moods go up and down; but my patience runs out. I get so upset at him. All he's been talking about lately is whether he should learn to play tennis, go back to golf, or start fishing again. I'm tired of hearing about how he is going to amuse himself next. Sometimes he seems to me to be like a small child, desperately searching for his favorite teddy bear."

"Well," Mary agreed, "In a sense he is searching for something."

"I know, I know," I said, "but it's so painful to watch him struggle and not be able to help."

"Well, I'm glad that you've finally realized that you can't solve his problems for him." Mary said.

"Yes," I agreed. "I guess I finally have faced that reality. All I can do is to give him my love."

"Except for prayer." she added. "Pray for him."

Pray, I mused, why pray? I had prayed before. Had it helped? I don't know. But what could I lose? There was no other way to turn. So I prayed. Off and on during the day and through many long hours at night I would ask God for help—for Mac and me.

How badly I wanted to escape the mad frantic world he was living in, but I couldn't. As I loved him, I not only shared his hopes and dreams but also his doubts and questions. It left me almost as bewildered as he. My anxiety was beginning to increase also for my mother. She had been sick and not responding to treatment. For six months she had been getting steadily worse. One day she called me from her home in Florida and said her doctor wanted to operate. Her voice was trembling as she went on to tell me about a tumor that had developed. I told her that as soon as I could make arrangements for the children I would come to see her.

Two days later I left—anxious and worried. I enjoyed flying, even though the trip from Minnesota to Florida was a long one, because it gave me time to think. High up in the clouds it seemed easier to look down upon my problems and the world in general. Away from the constant demands of the children, I could get a better focus on my life.

A child seated in front of me dropped a mirror from his mother's purse. When I reached over to pick it up for him, I noticed it was cracked and broken. I looked in it and was horrified to find my image covered with sharp, jagged, uneven lines. How like my life, I thought, whose problems were cracking the world around me and becoming more magnified every day. But not all of the lines were from the broken mirror as they were etched deeply into my forehead and under my eyes. Makeup could not cover the dark blue circles, and nothing could hide the strain in my eyes or the tightness in my face. When I handed him the mirror back, I tried to smile, and with a shock I realized how unnatural smiling had become to me.

As I looked down at the world beneath me—the

mighty Mississippi flowed like a narrow ribbon; winding through patches of greens and golds. I noticed a tiny speck which became a tug boat as I looked more closely and then saw a few more further on. Boats were going up and down the river. How many years had people navigated down that river, before I existed, and how many years would they continue after I had gone. Despite the hell that we go through here, life, like the river, still goes endlessly on and on and on. Oh God—I moaned in lonely silence—Why?

"Would you care for something to read?" The stewardess jarred me from my reverie. I thanked her and took a magazine.

"BISHOP PIKE'S DEAD SON RETURNS TO HIM" said the headline on the cover. Interested, I turned to the article and began to read as Pike described his communications through a medium with his son Jim. "My personality is the same now as it was before, but I am really more alive now because I don't have any physical problems. I am free!" Jim had told him.

The possibility of a life after death fascinated me. I knew I was not able to accept it as my own belief but curiosity had been incited. I'll have to read more about this I thought as I got off the plane.

Mother's surgery was the next day. It was shocking to see my youthful, attractive mother now gaunt and sallow and in such pain. Her clothes hung loosely on her withering body, and her skin had taken on a pale yellow cast as had the whites of her eyes. The seriousness of her situation came to me in a glance.

The operation seemed endless. It was nine hours before my stepfather and I were able to speak to the doctor. During that period we did not know if she was dead or alive. When it was time for our appointment with the doctor we were exhausted. Anxiously we began our long walk through a maze of subway tunnels that connected the hospital to the offices, hotels, shops, and clinic that all stemmed from the main building. The corridors were narrow and winding, branching off to the other halls and buildings. The walls were light green, normally a relaxing color if it weren't for the bright, shiny lights that stimulated our senses and dilated our pupils. There were many doors and signs to guide us. On and on we walked, opening and closing the doors. When we were not sure where to go we read the signs, asked questions, and sometimes made some wrong turns. How like the labyrinth of life, I thought, with the corners I had turned, the mistakes I had made, and the many doors that were still left for me to open. The sounds of footfalls on the tile floor were like heartbeats—tap, tap, tap. Some were steady and firm, others weak and faltering; new ones starting while others stopped, never to be heard again. Which door would I open? Which tap would I hear? Would the end of the footsteps here lead to a gate of eternal blackness, or would it open to another door of everlasting life?

We were there. We opened the last door. "I'm sorry," the doctor said, "the tumor was too large to remove. There is nothing we could do."

"Doctor," I asked. "How much time does she have

left?" From somewhere the answer came sharp and clear to my mind:
Four months!
The doctor's voice droned on in the background. "It's impossible for us to know or even guess the answer. Every case is different. From my many, many years of experience I would guess that it would be in terms of months rather than a year."

It did not matter to me what he said, for I had my answer—four months. From where, I did not know, but I knew with a very positive feeling that my mother would die around the first of April.

Mother accepted the idea of her short remaining time in life quietly and with ease. But I didn't. My stomach convulsed into knots. I couldn't eat. Tears streamed down my face and I felt angry—angry for her pain and her loss to me now, when I needed her comfort and advice so badly. I longed to be her little daughter again—not this lonely, isolated woman, anxious and lonely about a today filled with pain and a tomorrow I couldn't foresee. As I sat at her bedside I thought about death. It had been an unresolved question in my mind since my father's death when I was young. Now I was forced to think about it again. Death was something our society could not discuss easily—a morbid subject, shrouded under a veil of darkness and a dirge of tears. Was death a forever ending here, to be continued in a heaven abounding with celestial fluffy white angels with large ethereal wings, dancing on voluminous clouds of peace and eternal rest? Or perhaps

one could go the other way, into a pit of eternal hell and
damnation, fire and agony.

Mother said she was looking forward to a release from
her pain, and as I watched her in periods of deep sedated
sleep, I knew I could not wish her back into the world of
suffering. She was not afraid to die but seemed to have
developed an inner peace. In her lucid moments, we
discussed a life after death and the possibility that the
hereafter permitted communication with the soul
remaining, the same purportedly as Bishop Pike had
mentioned. This could leave open the possibility that the
hereafter not only permitted communication with other
loved ones but was filled with an active world of its own.
The further indication of Pike's son's communication to
him expanded the possibility that the spirit could and does
intermingle with our lives.

Mother mentioned that she had an uncle and
grandmother who had supposedly communicated with
spirits. No one in the family took them seriously. They
thought they were a little odd or senile. Maybe they were
right. But what if they weren't? What if they did
communicate with the dead? Was there really a life beyond
the one we are in now, one that we can know something
about? Mother wanted to believe. So did I, but I couldn't,
I just couldn't accept it. Oh, dear God, I prayed one night,
it would be so beautiful, so comforting if only I could
believe. Please help me to believe.

Her condition remained stable, so I returned home to
the demands of my busy household. Life with Mac was the

same as before. He would neither discuss nor think about Mother's pending death. The subject was too much for him to handle now. At times I felt him like a stranger, detached and removed from my needs and from the emotions of our family. I would reach out, but I could not feel him. He would not be there. Why, where had he gone? He was far away from us, I knew, deeply bottled up inside of himself, struggling with his own conflicts. I had become used to his unpredictable pattern, however, and even though I was riding the waves, I was not so worried about drowning. My mind needed to search for answers to its own questions. It had been challenged to Bishop Pike's article and I decided to read more.

I believed fortune telling, crystal balls, seances, gypsies with a crafty eye and a slippery hand, mysterious apparitions were all a lot of hocus pocus. The world was full of gullible people, suckers ready to be plucked for a dollar or two, or more by vultures waiting with a bag of clever tricks. Education had taught us to utilize all of our senses in probing the world around, and science trained us to test and retest our precepts; to weigh carefully, to analyze, scrutinize, calculate, to eliminate the emotional involvement, and to be objective. The theorems of math and science had guided many lives, including mine. As a graduate in Home Economics, I had received a Bachelor of Science Degree. In an age of superior scientific technology, the area of spiritualism seemed to me to be a part of the Black Ages. So I thought, until I began to check the book stores and found it very much a part of our own age. The occult department was growing daily with more and more books for an eager, awaiting public.

My library was expanding too as I began to investigate all phases of the occult. While I read, music from the song "AQUARIUS" blared out at me from the stereo. It promised the dawn of a new age—an age to abound with harmony and understanding, that love would steer the stars and peace would guide the planets. The time is right now, I thought, to open up our minds, to unfold, to expand, to toss away old concepts, and to have the courage to try the new and different. Perhaps it's time to stop fearing the unknown. Perhaps it's the time to investigate. Where would man be if he didn't try new things? Where would I be if I didn't?

The more I read, the more my skeptical mind began to open. I still had more questions and no real answers but instead an insight about God that I had never had before. I began to perceive the relationship between God and man as being a total integration—that God is in man too! Each of us has his own God power inside him. We must use this power to reach our fellow man, offering him love and help. By doing, we raise our own spiritual level to a greater fulfillment in the life beyond. By helping others we perfect ourselves. It seemed too simple to me, yet at times so difficult to achieve. My understanding of the hereafter was changing too. It appeared to me to be a further succession of our life—life as we know it now, but continuing on a different existence very similar but oh, so different. Death seemed more a continuance of life, moving from one sphere into another like when a person moves to another country and his environment changes. Was death that simple? A succession of life? A continuance of our present consciousness with a new environment and different opportunities to learn and develop? As we moved from life to afterlife, it appeared to be a natural time for reflection, and analysis, a perfect period to evaluate goals, reflect on mistakes and plan for future growth. Death just appeared to be a turning point in a continuance of life.

But how were our deeds rewarded and our debts paid? Where was our heaven and where was our hell? It appeared not to be as I had always been taught. For I learned when we wrong someone we lower our own level of consciousness and have to work our own way out through problems and suffering. We create our own hell by our own selfishness, then we must suffer the consequences. For all bad deeds are paid for eventually. By acts of love to our fellow man we raise our awareness and spiritual level to a far greater happiness and unification with our creator.

It sounded fair, so just and so right to me that even though my intellect knew that I could never accept these concepts as completely unquestionable truths, I was still filled with an estatic feeling of understanding and reason for being.

This was just another way of stating the truths that Christ taught us. But, don't we need the constant reminding to guide us down the course of life? We get involved with our worldly problems that sometimes we forget what it's all about. There are so many choices available to us that we waver, forget, and turn away from God. This basic philosophy seemed so beautifully simple, and as I read on, I discovered it was being expressed by many of our contemporary psychics.

Jeane Dixon is perhaps this country's best known psychic today. She was able to predict the assasinations of both Kennedys and the shooting of Martin Luther King. Her extraordinary gift of prophecy, combined with her deep religious faith, and the conviction that she uses her gift only to help mankind was very inspiring to me. I read about her in awe and wonderment. Her psychic abilities had grown and developed throughout her life. How badly I wanted to develop this too.

There were many books about Edgar Cayce that I read with fascination. Although he died in 1945 he is better known now than when he lived. Dozens of books and a library of information about his life and talents are available. When in a sleeping trance, Cayce's power of clairvoyance provided him with miraculous insights which went far beyond the realm of reality. Hundreds of people throughout the United States have testified to the accuracy of his diagnosis and treatment of illness that he practiced for 43 years. His readings, which were recorded while he was in a trance, provided fascinating information on the lost continent of Atlantis, E.S.P., dream analysis, and the lives of individuals who sought his help. What impressed me most about him was his sincere desire to help people.

Life was beginning to have meaning for me now and I began to investigate the various ways spirits communicated with mediums . . . automatic speech, automatic writing, ouija boards—it all seemed so strange to me. One day I found a book about automatic writing which was so compelling that I couldn't put it down until I had finished at three o'clock in the morning. In this form of communication the spirits, or guides as they are called, write through a person—using his hand as an instrument, giving messages from the world beyond. Could this really be true? Was imagination overiding reason? My rational mind refused to believe and yet something inside me kept pushing me on. Surely so many people could not lie. Could they all be wrong?

I had read many books by now, but there was one that I had not read for a long while—the best seller of all times—The Bible. It is a difficult book to read; the language is not ours and the meanings seem often contradictory. But, it is the Word of Christ, the greatest Teacher our world has known. The truth is there. I read on.

As I searched for Christ's testimony to us concerning life after death I realized that the story of his resurrection was an affirmation of the living soul. His demonstration of his own spiritual body during the great 40 days shows us that men experience a restoration to life soon after the death of the body, and always have done so. Christ, in human form as the Great Teacher, an example for us to follow, would not have come back if we could not do likewise in a lesser way. The cross thus becomes not an altar of vicarious sacrifice, as I have generally regarded it, but a part of the setting of a marvelous demonstration of the survival of the human soul after death. From St. Paul, Corinthians—Chapter 1, Epistle 1 read:

> "Behold, I show you a mystery. We shall not sleep,
> but we shall be changed."

How can this be unless man's being remains after
death? Christ saves men. Not only by his blood but by his
teaching doctrine and example. As in John XI Verse 63:

> "Now you are clean through the Word which I
> have spoken to you." "The words which I speak
> into you—they are spirit and they are life."

Thus, the only way to obtain the benefits of Christ's
divine mission is to try to live the Christ life of love, duty,
and service towards God and our fellow men.

He says there shall be work for us "as the angels of
God." If this is true, there will be plenty of work for us in
the afterlife. Finally free from the limitations and
sufferings of the human body; from the care and
maintenance of those who are dear to us; and from those
imperfections and weaknesses that are ours on earth, we
are free to devote ourselves to our better nature, to our
larger views and aspirations which were so difficult to
accomplish during our lifetime. We are able at last to be
reunited with those we love, to admire the wonders of
creation, and to take part in the wider work of the world.

The bible reminds us frequently of the angels and of
their roles in helping us. Acts, Chapter 27, Verse 23:

> "For there stood by me this night the Angel of
> God whose I am and whom I serve. Saying fear not
> Paul thou must be brought before Caesar and to
> God have given thee all them that sail with thee."

There appeared to be an extraordinary correlation
between the phenomena of ancient and of modern times.

The gift of prophecy, such as Jeane Dixon has, was repeated time and time again in the Bible. Had not prophets told of the birth of Christ? Had not the angel spoken to Mary about her giving birth to the Son? We read of the prophecies of Nahum, Habucus, Sophonias, and many others. Would these prophecies end with the death of Christ, or would they continue as his teachings did? Would it continue in personalities such as Jeane Dixon and Edgar Cayce? The truth appears to be that God sends his teachers in every age with revelations suited to the needs of the times. Jesus answers us in 1 Corinthians, Chapter 12:

> "Now concerning spiritual gifts, brethren, I would not have you ignorant. Now the manifestations of the spirit is given to everyone for profit. To one through the spirit is given the utterance of wisdom and to another the utterance of knowledge and to another faith, to another the gift of healing and in the same spirit, the working of miracles, to another speaking various kinds of tongues, to another interpreting those tongues and to another the distinguishing of all spirits. But all of these things are the work of one and the same spirit who allots to everyone according as he will."

Chapter 14:

> "Aim at charity, yet strive after the spiritual gifts, but especially that you may prophesy. He who prophesies speaks to men for edification and encouragement and consolation. He who prophesies edifies the church."

What wonderful gifts, I thought—and how blessed are those who receive them. But what about the strange

powers of automatic writing. It was difficult searching for
that, but when finally I came to Kings II I saw—

> "And there came a writing to him from Elijah the
> prophet saying, Thus saint the Lord God of David
> Thy Father" (this was several years after Elijah's
> death).

If the Bible is true, how can we doubt psychic
phenomena? For it is all in there, and it manifests itself in
many forms to demonstrate how to use the power and love
of God.

How did my church feel about this? Why has my
religion ignored this phenomenen? Are all of these things
really so strange or was it merely that they are not
commonplace? I had many questions.

The gifts of God have been many and great. I asked
God for one for myself. Oh God, help me to really believe
and understand this.

My reading and studying had to be
interrupted—Mother was getting worse. I visited her again
and as I saw her body eaten away by the insidious cancer, I
knew that death to her would be welcome. But when it
came it filled me with emptiness and loss. Something very
precious and beautiful had gone out of my life. A hollow
void was left inside me—my mother was gone.

"You were right," Mac said the day of the funeral.
"Your mother did die when you said she would." I went
to the calendar and counted the time from that fateful day
in the doctor's office until she died. It was four months.

"How did you know?" he said.

"I don't know," I answered. "I just heard it—it just

came popping through my head."

Why? How? I didn't know.

"It was a premonition I guess. I can't understand it. I only know it happened." My mind began to reflect on some of the famous psychic personalities I had been reading about who could fortell future events. Maybe, just maybe, I had some of this ability too.

But I was tired now. I felt the strain I had been under, with both Mac and mother. I just wanted to rest; to sit back and not worry about anyone else anymore; to find peace and quiet somewhere.

"Hey, Mom, I need some new clothes, everything's too small." "Mom, when are we going to eat?" "Mom, can I invite eight kids to my birthday party?" "Mom, will you take me to the library?"

"Mom, mom, mom," rang through the house, starting at six o'clock when Jimmy awoke until ten o'clock at night when Kevin finally went to bed. It was a mixed blessing to be needed. Love I had. Quiet I didn't have and rest was not for me.

It was early morning when Mac awakened me. Light had begun to filter through the blue draperies to highlight his face. When he sat down next to me on the bed I noticed his anxious troubled eyes. It frightened me. I jumped up and asked, "What's the matter?"

"I'm sorry to wake you but I have something to tell you. I want you to know that some day I might have to leave you and the children. It's not because I don't love you but I have something important to do."

I had heard it before and the words had never left me, but now as I listened to them again, chilling shivers went up and down my back. My body began to perspire profusely.

"But—but—" I said.

"I can't tell you any more. I don't know any more. That's all."

"That's all?" I shudered. Could this be another premonition? I stared into his sad eyes and wondered what tomorrow would bring.

Gone Was the Stranger

"You've got to be out of your mind to read this, and if you're not now, you soon will be," Mac said as he picked up one of the books I had been reading. "MANIFESTATIONS OF THE DEAD. For God's sake why do you read this? You've got books piled beside your bed, stacked in the living room, and you even read while you cook dinner. It's hard to do, but you do it. I think you're cracking up."

"Hey look, don't take my word—read it yourself!" I argued. "Psychic phenomena is fascinating. How can you criticize it when you don't know anything about it?" He thumbed through the pages of one of the books and didn't seem to hear me.

Yes, why? I thought to myself. Why? am I digging into this subject so intensely? There seems to be a hunger

inside of me, compelling me to search. But search for
what. Did I really want to believe and prove what I had
been learning, or was I trying to find a meaning for my
own life?

"Look at this one," he said, as he handed me a book,
"pictures of ghosts! You're being conned. Someone's
making money off of people like you. There is a sucker
born every day. Ghost stories are fine for kids, but you're
a little old for that. When I was about twelve I became
interested in ghosts myself. I'll never forget the night Tom
and Dan and I sneaked out of our rooms after our folks
had gone to bed. Tom had taken a package of cigarettes
from his dad's drawer. We thought we'd hide behind the
garage and have a lesson in the fine art of cigarette
smoking, but he ripped his pants in climbing from his
bedroom window and got so shook up that he forgot to
get matches. There we were, the three of us, sitting in the
alley and trying to decide what to do with a package of
cigarettes and no matches. Dan was giggling at Tom who
was trying to come up with an explanation for his ripped
pants. 'Gee Mom I didn't notice. My pants torn? Musta
happened in the washing machine.' We were sitting right in
back of Old Lady Cannonball's house. Now we all knew
that Old Lady Cannonball was pretty wierd. She lived
alone in a tiny house that looked like a summer cottage.
When she would hobble down the street, cane in hand,
wearing a long black skirt and an old holey lavender
sweater, a frilly bonnet tied neatly under her chin, we
stared in wonderment. We had never seen anyone so old in
our lives. Her face was wrinkled up like a prune while her

nose jutted out, long and pointed. We figured she must be over a hundred. Whenever she would see us, she would yell in a crackly, shaky voice 'You leave me alone or I'll call the police, ya hear?' The stories had been going around in the neighborhood lately that her house was haunted! 'Hey, Dan,' I said, 'did Suzy tell you about the ghost she heard at Old Lady Cannonball's house last night? They were moaning and groaning and no one was there. The light kept going off and on, and Old Lady Cannonball wasn't even home.'

'Bullshit!' Tom replied.

'No shit!' I answered in affirmation.

"There was only one thing to do. The three of us appointed ourselves a ghost hunting party, and we climbed over the fence and into her backyard. There was no moon that night, so it was very dark. We couldn't even see each other and we were scared! The giggling had stopped and was replaced by heavy, expectant breathing. Tom decided to crawl along the ground to get closer to the house. Dan thought he'd follow, when all of a sudden a loud shrill cry pierced the night. Then another and another! A scrambling of bodies was heard—a scratching, thumping and then that awful cry again. We took off over the fence. Oops! Tom caught the leg of his pants on the post and it ripped. We sat in the alley, panting and shaking, wondering what to do next. Tom was surveying the damage on his pants, when two big black cats leaped over the fence and were gone in the night. Have you ever heard a cat fight? Wow!"

"Great story," I grumbled. "But I'm not reading just about ghosts. It's more about a philosophy of life. Don't be so closed-minded—read some of these things and see for yourself."

"Hell, I don't have time. Besides I am more concerned with what is happening now. And so should you be."

I realized that nothing I could say would convince Mac that psychic phenomena might be real. His laughing at my interest hurt me, so I kept my thoughts to myself and read when he was not around—but I knew that someday he would be exposed to a psychic experience. That night, in prayer, I asked God that Mac be given some sign that would open the door to his believing. There were so many things that I wanted to share with him. It was a few weeks later that he called me from the office . . .

"Judy, I've got a ghost story for you."

"Oh, come on now, Mac," I said, "I'm not interested in any more of your stories."

"No, I'm not kidding. I think this might be a real one. A couple came into the office today. They had just sold a farm and had some money to invest. I took them out to lunch and happened to ask them why they left the farm. They hesitated at first, and said that one of the reasons was because it was haunted. I'll tell you about it when I get home tonight." Now I was the skeptical one.

"Is it dark enough for your ghost story? Shall we light a campfire and you can hold my hands while you tell it to me?" I said after the children had gone to bed.

"O.k., o.k.,—you can laugh if you want but, these ghosts have some possibility."

"I'll try you again, but it better be good," I said.

"Well, Carol and Chuck, who owned the farm were a little nervous at first about being so far out in the country, as Chuck worked nights in the city. But, after they moved in Carol said she did not feel alone. It was a strange thing, but she felt there was always someone with her. Then they began to notice strange noises in the house. They knew there had to be some explanation and assumed it was their cats. But when they put the cats in the barn, they still had the noises. The mystery was developing for them, and they began to check out every strange noise they heard, but couldn't find a source. At Christmastime they heard the sounds of an electric train. Carol said they could hear the click, clack as if wheels rolled on the tracks and the sound it makes as it goes through the tunnel. It sounded just like a toy train. One day the children asked them when they could play with the train they heard every night. But, there wasn't a train in the house or anywhere nearby. A woman came to visit one day, she told them she had stayed overnight in the house before they had owned it. 'Tell me,' she asked, 'do you ever hear the sound of a toy train in the house?' I guess that really convinced them that the noises were not a part of their imaginations.

"Chuck said that what really satisfied his feelings that the house was haunted was when he came into the living room and saw the rocking chair moving very fast as if someone had just been sitting in it. He hurriedly ran through the room and out the door. As he turned the corner to the next room, an extremely tall, older man was standing in front of him. He stood there for what seemed like an hour but probably was only seconds, and then this man disappeared right in front of him. He did not turn and walk away but literally evaporated. He called the previous owner of the house and questioned her about her parents who had built the house and lived there. She said they had died twenty years ago, and as she described her father's appearance, Chuck said he really began to shake, because it was exactly like the man he had seen. He saw 'him' again one morning while milking cows. 'He' was patting a cow on the back. Later, Chuck said he could sense when 'he' was around, because the cows would suddenly become quiet and contented. That ghost sure must have had a way with cows."

"Did the woman ever see him?" I asked.

"Well, by this time," Mac said, "I was really fascinated. I asked Carol that same question. She said one day she was working in the living room, when she heard a voice behind her saying, "Well, you can do this if you want to, but I'm going outside." She turned and saw the figure of a woman who was clothed in a high-neck dress with tiny buttons down the front and long sleeves. The image was clear at first, then became hazy and finally disappeared completely. They said they could have talked for hours about 'their ghosts' but our lunch was over. I asked them how it felt to share a home with spirits as we left, and they both agreed that for the most part they were not bothered by their presence, and were even grateful for the experience, because it gave them a religious conviction that death is not to be feared and that the spirit does survive."

"That's a better ghost story than the first one you told me," I laughed. "But I can't really be convinced that this is true either."

"Well, neither can I. I guess the only way I could really believe it is if I were to experience it myself. I have no reason to doubt these people. They are intelligent, realistic, and very normal. If there is any truth at all to this, it certainly opens up some interesting speculations."

"Hmmmmm." I murmurred with a knowing smile on my face.

"O.K., maybe you're right. Just maybe—" he conceded.

While Mac no longer complained when I read my "crazy books," he still reflected the turmoil that pervaded his world. That driving force that spewed and spun him from pinnacles of enlightenment into inky catacombs of desperation remained. The fear of "the something he wanted to do" never left me. I lay awake at night worrying that it might be a warning or premonition. I kept praying for him—for us. It was my only hope. And when I did, I thought of him as a happy person. I closed my eyes and visualized Mac and me as happy. What was the happiest time of our life together? Our wedding day, I thought. I concentrated deeply on the happiness we shared then and asked that it be returned to us. I kept this picture in my mind often during the days and the lonely hours of the night. Many, many times in the simple plea of a woman in need of help, I asked God that joy be returned to us and that Mac be given the guidance he needed to find his role in life and the significance that he wanted so desperately.

Slowly, very slowly I began to see a change in him. A flickering ray of hope had appeared. Spring was with us now, and as the tulips and daffodils pushed from the cold, dark ground to signal their resurrection, I too felt a surge of promise and optimism. The warm weather stimulated me and I was eager to get outdoors and explore what the long icy winter had hidden.

I suggested to Mac that it would be fun to take a short camping trip and he agreed. It seemed to me a good way to pull him back into the family fold. Besides, the stock market had reached a point of steady decline and an economical diversion would be welcome.

But getting ready for the trip was work. There were times when I thought I must have lost my mind to take seven people camping. The packing and repacking seemed to go on forever: food, tent, sleeping bags, flashlights, cook stove, lanterns, clothes for warm weather, clothes for cold weather, clothes for rainy weather, books, magazines, and most important—insect repellant. The list seemed to get longer every time we went.

We're all set to go! Oops! "Dad can we go fishing?" In goes the outboard motor, tackle box, life jackets, and fishing rods.

"Now, everyone in?" One more trip to the bathroom and we are off. "The dogs!" "What shall we do with the dogs?" Mike asked. Pets, we had learned by experience, can have an unpleasant time when they tangle with wild animals such as skunks and porcupines. That was one problem I didn't care to deal with. Off went the dogs to the neighbors! And off we went to the north woods!

It was the first camping trip for Jimmy. I had not had the desire to hassle with the problems of infancy in the woods, but now that he was three we were eager to have him with us. He was quite a sport! His amusing comments, bright-eyed expressions, and contagious laughter made life without him seem quite dull. He could sleep wherever he might fall and his naps were taken in the car, curled up on the floor or sometimes slumped over the toilet seat. There was a big, exciting creation outdoors for Jimmy to see, to smell, and to touch, and watching him explore it was thrilling. It was like seeing anew through the expansive, inquisitive mind of a child. The world was waiting for Jimmy.

Probably the biggest thrill of camping is when you drive into the forest, get out of the car, and take a big, deep breath. The fresh, sharp, clean air, fragrant with the smell of pine, enters your nostrils and permeates your whole body, invigorating and stimulating you. Oh, if it could only be bottled up and taken home! The tall, stately pines, reached to the sky and formed walls of thick trees. At night the campfires and hanging lanterns made our forest home look like a castle, with soft, golden lights blinking and flickering and shadows dancing back and forth.

It was good to break away from the routine and venture out into new experiences. It was delightful not to be plagued by the ringing phones and noises of the city. Instead we heard the music of the wind rustling through the trees. The scampering of chipmunks, and birds singing around us. It was fun to free ourselves from the routine and mechanization of daily living and open up to whatever might happen next—maybe just to sit and stare at the dying embers of the campfires and let thoughts come drifting in and out. It was a time to think, a time to play, a time to relax, or a time to just curl up and let the world drift around us.

Mac loved to poke around the fire, which was going all of the time because the nights were chilly and the days were spent eating. I smiled as I saw him standing there adding logs to feed the flame. The smoke curled around him and the soot darkened his old army shirt and blackened his face. He looked relaxed and content, and the angry lines were gone. It had been so long since I had seen him like that.

The children were excited about everything they saw. They made toy furniture from moss and built homes out of leaves and twigs. How much fun they had discovering wild berries and beautiful flowers growing all around us. The berries were saved for pancakes and the flowers decorated our table. Every pocket was filled with "precious" stones that would be brought home to their dresser drawers to stay "forever"; good memories like that just couldn't be thrown away. The chipmunks amused us all: small, fast, friendly little creatures with big brown eyes that were forever searching for food. We spent hours feeding and trying to catch them. What delightful pastime!

The campgrounds had many interesting trails to explore and off the children went, screaming, running, and chasing each other. Jimmy fell. His chubby legs could not keep up, but Kevin scooped him up in his arms and plopped him on his shoulders and ran to catch up with the others. We sighed in relief. "I hope they burn off a little of that energy," Mac said. "Hey, lets take a walk just by ourselves."

We headed toward the lake. The sun was bright and warm now, and we decided to stretch out on the soft sand and enjoy the quiet. The brilliant blue sky, the white sand, and steady rhythm of the lapping waves reminded me of the beautiful beach in South Carolina where we had begun our marriage thirteen years ago. So many years had gone by, yet it seemed as if only a day had passed. Where had that time gone?

I looked at Mac. The years had been good to him. As he stretched out on the beach, I laughingly called him Adonis, the Greek god. His physique was strong and trim; and he was still young, healthy, and vital. The angry person I had lived with for the past two years was gone. The man I had loved and married was back again. As we strolled along the beach, his arm around my shoulder, there was no anger in his eyes. No hostility. Gone was the stranger.

"Tweetie," he said, "I'm happy."

He hadn't used that name in years and it went perfectly with the hug of his arms around my shoulder. I began to cry and as his arms went around me, my sobs engulfed us and convulsed my body, as though it were trying to shake away those horrible memories of lonliness and despair. They gave way now to thoughts of other nights . . . nights when we lay naked, warm, and at peace.

There would be that tonight.

The kids burst through the woods and found us in warm embrace. The quiet was shattered now, but its peace remained with us. Hand in hand, we followed them back to the campsite.

The next day the temperature dropped. A north wind promised cold and rain. A warm house appealed to us all. Our adventure was over, and we began to pack up our things and get ready to leave.

"Hey, just a minute," Mac said. "We can't go until we have Campers Awards."

Mac and I had a short conference, and then he whistled for the campers to line up in front of "Big Mac" to receive their awards for merit and bravery in the wilderness.

Jimmy's award as funniest camper was unquestioned: his speculation that "chipped" (chipmunks) look like "broked squirrels" would have won him the title, but he cinched it when he mentioned his concern over the "crumbs" from the firecrackers falling in his hair.

Mary received her award for catching the most fish, and certainly father deserved something for baiting hooks. After twenty, we lost count of the baby sunfish that six-year old Mary hauled in with squeals of delight.

Michael, our dreamer, was lost in another world of thought when Kevin put a dead Muskie on the end of his line. Was Mike surprised when he thought he had captured this big, ugly fish! Even though the stench was pretty bad, he still received the award for the largest catch.

Kathleen won top citation for her noble concern for the animal kingdom. I'm sure the stomach of every chipmunk within a mile radius is still full from her feeding them popcorn, peanuts, and crackers. It's no wonder we ran out of food.

Kevin got the "biggest swinger" award. Something always happens when Kevin is around. He is a "wheeler and dealer", a planner, promoter, agitator, coordinator, and general hanky panky artist. He's responsible for many laughs, fights, and much excitement. We always felt relief when he would take down the road for a visit with some newly made friends, giving us a chance to rest up for what he would do next.

Back home, as I ran the washing machine for the sixth time and removed the sand, stones, dried flowers, and squished berries from the pockets, smelling the last of the smoke as it went down the drain, I thought, yes, it was worth it! And it was.

It was late August now—still warm but dry, with the grass turning brown, the mosquitoes reaching gargantuan size, and the children just a little bit bored with summer activities and each other. My days were busy getting the children's clothes ready for school. We had one last weekend before the busy school year crowded in upon us and summer was over.

Sunday Mac and Reyn went sailing. It was the last race of the season and they hoped to make up for their bad record. Mary and I took all of the children and went to the lake to watch. It was a beautiful day with the wind blowing the sails hard. Suddenly the rope that Mac was holding broke, and into the lake he went, catching his pants on a hook. Mary and I burst into laughter as we saw Mac scrambling to get back into the boat, with the whole seat of his pants torn out.

"They're just like little boys". Mary said. "It's good to see Mac like this. He's so much more relaxed than he was."

"Yes he is," I said, "but still, I have the feeling that he is resting up for something—. Sometimes I think that he is building up his strength for something important—."

"I lost my good smoker," Mac said, as he came up to us, trying to hold his pants together and carry the sails at the same time. "Damn it, I think most of my pipes are at the bottom of that lake. We'd better get home before I get picked up for indecent exposure."

"Let's go for a ride by ourselves," Mac said after dinner that night. I got the younger children settled, put Kevin in charge for a few hours and went out to the car to wait for him. He always had some last minute problem: "who took my key?" or, "where is my pipe?" I got into his little sports car and waited. He came out of the house and down the stairs. He was wearing his "play clothes," as I called them; the clothes he laughed, played and felt comfortable in—a navy striped T shirt that I had given him for Father's Day, denim bell bottom pants and leather Mexican sandals. A flash went through my mind: "That's what he will be buried in."

"How ridiculous!" I gasped. The thought was gone.

But like a voice, it came again. "The funeral—it will be him." I was shaken. I looked at him getting into the car, healthy, happy, vital, and alive. No! I couldn't believe it! I rejected it. I forgot it. Off we went in the car, the wind blowing in our faces and the radio blaring in our ears.

"Let's go see if Al and Patty are home."

"Good idea," I said.

Al Currier, a minister, had been in Europe all summer. He had once had a parish in Germany for five years, and his heart was still with the people of Europe and their struggle for freedom. That evening we had been talking about the problems of Europe and the rest of the world when Al suddenly piped up with, "say, Zorba, remember the night you did THE LORD OF THE DANCE?" My Irishman had a habit of dancing after alcohol had been bubbling in his veins for awhile. The music would be loud, his legs would start to move, and off he would go like a wind-up toy that couldn't be stopped. He had just enough ham in him, enough comedian, and enough strong drink to put on a good show. Al loved to call Mac, Zorba the Broker, in reference to the main character in the movie Zorba the Greek, a free spirit who would whirl round and round until he would fall to the floor in exhaustion, only to bounce back up and dance again. The role of Zorba the Greek was a sharp contrast to the stereotyped stockbroker image. It was a strange combination role that Mac played: the unconventional maverick character of Zorba trying to meet the conformist requirements of the financial world. It became a dichotomy in him that pulled him back and forth, up and down, just like the dance. THE LORD OF

THE DANCE was a new one that I hadn't seen yet. I really didn't have to; I knew what it would be like.

It was still early when we left Al and Patty's, so we decided to take a drive. We seemed to be surveying the past, I thought, as we circled the neighborhoods where we had grown up, saw the schools we attended and the homes we had lived in. Nothing looked very different—just like us, a little bit older.

"Let's stop to see your folks," I said. We didn't get to see them very often, and when we did, the children would be climbing all over them, making it difficult to talk. They were still awake, so we chatted for awhile and then left for home. It had been a full day, but a beautiful one. We both flopped into bed, relaxed and contented with the world.

"Judy, I talked to Chuck again today. You know who I mean? The one with the ghosts in the house?"

"Yes, I know the one. Don't tell me you have another ghost story?"

"No, but he told me a few other things. You might be right about a life after death. By the way, I lost a big order today that I needed very badly. I think I'll stay downtown tonight."

"I wish you would come home," I said. It was Monday. What a way to start the week, I thought. The bars of the city were no place to handle disappointment and frustration.

"I'm sorry. I just don't want to."

"I'm sorry too. Good-by." Will he ever learn, I

thought, as I hung up the phone? Will that damn Irishman ever learn that drinking with the boys is not going to solve his problems?

"Come on kids, let's eat dinner. Daddy's not coming home tonight."

We had a light dinner, then I went to bed early. The phone's shrill ring on the table next to my bed awakened me. I looked at the clock. It was 12:30.

"Mrs. McCarthy?" the voice asked.

"Yes," I mumbled sleepily.

"This is St. Paul-Ramsey Hospital calling. Your husband has been in an accident. Can you come right away?"

"Yes, Yes," I answered. "I'll be right there. Can you tell me how he is?"

"I'm sorry. The doctor will have to talk to you."

I put down the phone and picked it up again. I needed help. I dialed Mary and Reyn's number. Reyn's voice answered. "Please take me to the hospital," I said, "It's Mac."

"I'll be right over," Reyn said.

I woke Kevin and told him that I had to go out for awhile. He mumbled something and went back to sleep.

Reyn was there in minutes. I ran to the car. "I don't know anything," I said.

"What did they say?"

"Just that it was an accident. They wouldn't tell me anything more. I'm really scared. It's no good. Poor Mac."

"We don't know anything yet. It could be nothing," Reyn said as he drove faster.

"It's no good." Was my only reply, as I prayed silently during the rest of the ride—"Oh God, please help him."

We walked into the sterile, antiseptic atmosphere of the emergency room, the cold bright lights glaring in our faces. In the background white uniformed figures scurried back and forth, as if in automation, while people dressed in street clothes stood waiting and watching, crying or staring blankly into space. I approached a nurse and gave her my name. Faces turned to look at me, then hurriedly looked away.

"Can you please tell me—" I begged.

"This way please. The doctor will speak to you." The crisp voice interrupted.

She took us to an elevator and pushed a button. We rode in silence. The elevator door opened. She walked out. "Wait here, I will get the doctor." As we stood in the bare, grey hall, a priest came toward us, dressed in black, solemn and ominous, his beads around his neck and a prayer book in his hand. He tried to speak, but backed quickly away as the white figure came back again.

"This is Dr. Olson, Mrs. McCarthy."

"Mrs. McCarthy, your husband is dead." A voice said. "He was killed almost instantly. He was dead when he arrived here. I'm sorry. There was nothing we could do."

I heard. The words came pounding again, again, and again. Your husband is dead. Your husband is dead . . . Nothing we could do . . . Killed instantly . . . Dead Dead . . . Dead.

It was all over. Mac was gone.

A white figure beckoned. On the elevator we went. Down . . . down . . . down . . . Dead . . . dead . . . Mac was dead.

"You may step over here please to get his belongings." A white voice said. I wrote my name on something and was handed a bag. A brown bag. I came to the hospital for Mac and returned with a brown bag. A brown bag that held a watch and a billfold.

Empty . . . hollow . . . helpless. It was all over. There was nothing I could do.

Reyn and I got back into the car and drove over to tell Mac's folks and then home to the children. "Oh God, those poor children," I said.

Composure came over me, as I walked into Kevin's room. Strength seemed to be emanating from somewhere.

"Kevin, Kevin," I said. I shook him awake gently.

"Kevin, listin to me carefully." My voice was calm, soothing, shaky but controlled. "Daddy was just killed in an automobile accident." Kevin stared at me in shock, trying to wake up, yet wanting to go back to sleep to shut out the nightmare. "He didn't suffer Kev; he died quickly. He's going to be happy now," I said. "Christ promised us happiness after death, and daddy will be happy. He was a good man. A very good man. Daddy had a lot of problems here that he doesn't have anymore. His spirit is free now, free to do important things that he couldn't do when he was here. He loved us before, Kev, and he won't stop loving us now. It's true that we won't be able to see him, but he will still be with us, watching over and helping us when we need him. You musn't feel sorry for him Kev," I said. "Daddy enjoyed life, and he will be happy now. Christ has told us that," I repeated. "Kevin, don't worry about us. We'll manage. We can do it." I spoke with strong conviction, feeling the truth of everything I said.

One by one, I talked to the children. They stared in disbelief, and they cried. But slowly they accepted and understood and felt what I felt.

The house was filled with confusion and activity when the newspapers and television picked up the story of the accident, and people got the news. Neighbors and friends came in and took over for me. They helped with the children, washed clothes, prepared food, managed the household for me. The true church and spirit of Christianity surrounded us, as people came from all over to give their help.

I slept very little and I ate nothing, but I felt very strong and confident. Overpowering, overwhelming feelings of understanding came over me, as I lay in the big, cold double bed, all alone. Mac, I thought, you're happy now. I can't feel sorry for you. Now you have returned to the everloving God who put you on this earth, who can give you much greater happiness than I could. Is it not the true test of love to be able to give up a loved one, so that they can share in a greater love and happiness? I gave him to God and felt a glowing joy within myself, a peace of mind I had never known before. I knew I must not feel sorry for myself: self pity is negative. It pushes you back, and I couldn't go back. For the children's and my sake I couldn't and can't go back, but must go forward and find a new life for all of us. Emotions of joy and understanding kept me buoyed up, and when I saw the tears of sobbing friends, I could comfort them. If only they could feel what I was feeling. If only they could know. But they didn't know, and they thought that I was in shock or didn't realize what had happened. But I knew death only too well. It was no stranger to me. It had taken my mother and my father and now my husband. I knew it well.

It came back to me, when the mortician asked what Mac should wear for his funeral. I had almost forgotten what that strange voice had told me three days before. "The casket will be closed," I said. "He will wear the clothes he loves." I went to the closet and got his blue denim bell-bottoms, his navy blue striped T-shirt, and his Mexican sandals.

"The funeral—it will be him." Yes, I knew. The funeral will have to be of love, joy, dedication to humanity. It will be an affirmation of Mac.

The sun was shining brightly. It was a lovely, warm day. The hearse pulled up in front of the church. Friends and relatives were standing, waiting on the church lawn. They were singing, "They will know we are Christians by our love." The singing was led by a beautiful soprano voice, and accompanied by the guitars that Mac loved so much.

Father George Garrelts set the tone for the funeral
mass. He motioned to the people to sit down. In his calm,
relaxed voice he said, "I know that Jim would like you to
be comfortable. Please have a seat and join us."

The music was Mac. It was me. The music was the
way I felt, the way I believed. I sang out, long and clear.

Of my hands I give to you O Lord
Of my hands I give to you
I give to You as You gave to me,
Of my hands I give to you.
Of my heart I give to you O Lord
Of my heart I give to you
I give to You as You gave to me;
Of my heart I give to you.
Of my life I give to you O Lord
Of my life I give to you
I give to You as You gave to me;
Of my life I gave to you.

I had asked Al Currier to speak.

"Now abideth faith, hope and love, and the greatest
of these is love." In a voice rich and deep, vibrant with
emotion, he sang, *The Lord of the Dance* that Mac had
danced to such a short time ago.

"I danced in the morning when the world was begun,
And I danced in the moon and stars and the sun,
And I came down from heaven and I danced on the
earth
At Bethlehem I had my birth.

Dance then wherever you may be
I am the Lord of the Dance said he
And I'll lead you all wherever you may be
I'll lead you all in the dance, said he.

I danced on a Friday when the sky turned black
It's hard to dance with the devil on your back.
They buried my body and they thought I'd gone
But I am the dance and I still go on."

The room was breathlessly silent now but penetrating through the stillness a tense mixture of passionate emotions vibrated. Why? What? Silence. Suddenly, Al's loud voice cut through the expectancy. "Jim is dead. Zorba the Broker isn't at his desk. Lids have been lowered over the eyes that laughed with the light of the leprechaun. Stillness steals in, cutting the cacophony of life with the sobriety of death. It cuts the curtains of cackling conversaion. It insulates us from the onslaught of incidentals, and leaves us alone, terribly alone. The silence stabs until our lives become quiet enough to hear the flute of faith. Not knowledge. Not certainty. We can't see it, catch it, touch it, or test it. It's the Pied Piper of love playing across Palestine. It's Jim, questioning the faith with his lips and affirming it with his life. It's the trumpet of Easter's triumph sounding beyond the horizon of our comprehension. It's the song of faith, the symphony of life, sounding in the silence of our sorrow."

He sang again, so loud that I trembled:

"Sing then wherever you may be
I am the Lord of life said he
And I'll lead you all wherever you may be
I'll lead you all in the dance said he."

His voice was low and quiet. He talked on . . .

"Few of us have drunk the dregs of despair, wept for the wounds of our brothers, or been hunted by the hound of heaven like Jim. The faces of the the faceless starving in Biafra were burned in his soul. He cursed the constraint of convention to cry out against the bitter bloodshed in Vietnam. He called to the conscience of his country, the commandments of Christ, and the crisis of youth, when he put his arms around the Milwaukee Fourteen. He was a white-black and a black-white. He wrestled with the wrongs of the wrongs of the world, wept with the wretched, marched with the militant; he comforted the troubled and troubled the comfortable. He wrestled, wept, and fought, because he dared to hope.

The heart of his hope was the love he knew . . . the love of God that carried him when his conscience condemned him . . . the love of those he most deeply loved. Because of love, he loved to live and he lived to love. And the love he lived cannot die. It burns in the heart of his wife and beats in the blood of his family. His love of life and life of love has splashed over and baptized all who knew him. It flows in and floods the silence of our sorrow with faith, hope, and love.

It is the trumpet behind the triumph of the mass.
It is the tamborine of the Lord of the Dance."

Al sang out again, his voice throbbing with feeling, to a powerful finale.

> "They cut me down and I leap up high
> I am the life that'll never never die,
> I'll live in you if you'll live in me
> I am the Lord of the Dance said he."

Al, you did it! You did it! You who had known him as no one else knew him; you who had suffered, cried, and struggled with him. Only you could have done that. It was beautiful. The funeral—it was Mac.

I felt very proud of him, as I followed his casket out of the church, and stepped into the shiny, black limousine. Many thoughts rushed through my mind during the short ride. Was it that Mac cared too much for people that made it so difficult for him to cope with life's brutal realities? Was it because of his penetrating sensitivity that he tried too hard to solve all of life's problems? Perhaps a man's ultimate failure is in not trying at all. But, Mac had tried. And in trying he had succeeded. For, in trying, he had touched many lives and left with them the message of Christ—that he cared for them.

The branches of a small tree waved in the warm afternoon sun next to a deep, rectangular pit in freshly turned black soil. Slowly, very slowly, I walked toward the hole, then knelt beside the big bronze casket. With tears streaming down my face, I picked a white rose from his grave then walked away in silence.

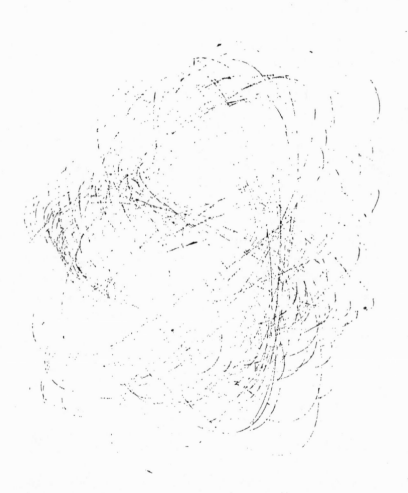

Page 3313

The house was quiet again—quiet and dirty! Relatives, friends, and neighbors had all left. Unwashed clothes were stacked up, the vacuum cleaner had broken, the lawn mower didn't work, the car wouldn't start, and a pile of unpaid bills lay threateningly on Mac's desk. How, I wondered, can I handle everything with my income cut in half?

From habit, I picked up the white rose and stuck it into a glass of water.

Then I took my first real look in the mirror since the accident. My face was drawn and thin, the skin parched and itching—dehydrated from my having lost 15 pounds in a week! My stomach rebelled at the thought of food. Even a glass of milk was hard for me to swallow. I felt as though I was recovering from major surgery, and I guess I really was, for a part of me had been ripped away, and my body ached from exhaustion at the loss. To merely walk across the room required an energy I didn't have. As I sat and slowly sipped some tea, I began to realize that it would take me a long, long time before I had healed from the shock that death had left with me. Rest, sleep, food and time would help, but now I felt weak and so very old. Like an aged woman, my poor aching body begged for rest.

I glanced up at the Christmas portrait of the children and became engulfed by the responsibility that lay ahead for me to raise them all alone, but as I looked at each of them I began to see how much they gave to me. Kevin, with maturity beyond his twelve years, was out cutting the lawn. The grass didn't really need to be cut now, but today he needed to cut it. As he sat at the head of the table at night, he took his father's role—and he did it well. He had a strong shoulder for me to lean on, but his childhood was over now.

Kathleen's pretty, sweet face smiled at me in the picture, and it mirrored her attitude toward life, for wherever she walked there was beauty and kindness—with lots of giggles built in. It was fun to watch her grow and to share in her girlhood delights.

Perhaps Michael would fulfill some of Mac's dreams, I thought, as I stared at his handsome, freckled face that was so much like his father's, for he too had a compassionate feeling for others.

Mary with her funny, bouncy ways, gave to me her joy of living, something I needed so badly but could only appreciate now vicariously.

But Jimmy, he was the one! With infancy still reflecting in his chubby face, he held the symbol of hope. For Jimmy, still a baby, represented birth and the continuance of life. With thoughts of death hovering so close to me, Jimmy's innocence and dependence kept me closely attuned to life.

I am surrounded by lots of love and vitality, I thought, and these children will become a part of my healing force. What I have to give to them is the confident assurance that life will continue, and I will have to be constantly prepared to meet their emotional needs. Together the six of us will rebuild our lives—somehow—some way.

What overwhelmed me the most though, was my own attitude. Since the hour of Mac's death, I seemed to be bombarded by emotional strength and positive feelings. I had an overpowering certainty that everything was going to be all right with myself and the children. I knew that I had nothing to worry about. It was true that my life would be dramatically changed, but I believed it would involve adjusting to new roles and situations which could be challenging and exciting to me, if I cared to make them that way. I felt free from problems and worries. I knew that everything was going to be all right now. As I recalled my premonitions of Mac's death, I knew that it was meant to be, for he had done all that he could do on this earth. He had opened up new channels of thought and had instigated a responsibility to subsequent action in many people. The dedication Mac felt to alleviate the problems of society would be carried on by those he inspired.

Although his stay in this world was short, it had brought meaning and dimension to many. His goals would not be forgotten but would be fulfilled through others.

When the world in which he lived oppressed him beyond his endurance he had left it for far greater happiness. I remembered the words that he had told me twice: *Judy, there's something I have to tell you. You're not going to understand, but some day I'm going to have to leave you and the children. It's not because I don't love you, but because I have something important to do.* Whether these words were precognitive or not, I did not know. But now I understood them.

I radiated in the happiness that was with him now. He was free from the physical anxieties that had tormented him. No longer did he have a job that frustrated him. No longer did he have to worry about the market going up or down. No longer did he have to worry about the escapes that tormented him. Instead, he was able to pursue the goals which his spirit had longed for. What freedom! What genuine freedom he now had—a freedom he had so desperately longed for here. With this freedom came a far greater happiness, a knowledge of God that mortals do not have.

I was well aware of the responsibilities and obligations I had ahead of me. I knew that it was up to me to fulfill them. I felt that what had happened to me must be used to strengthen myself, my children, and the people around me. For me, life must be a continuous process of either growing or shrinking. I could let myself be swallowed up, drowned in the dregs of self-pity, or I could choose to thrive with the enormous strength and powers given to me. Should I dilute or weaken the graces which were coming to me with negative feelings of sorrow and grief? Shouldn't I try to remove those feelings by my earnest desire to do so and with the help of God? I knew that negativism comes from oneself and that positiveness comes from God. I chose to be positive—to grow.

This was the faith that I had once questioned, but now I knew. This is the faith I was now living and it would give to me a new life.

Mac would not leave us. I knew that. As he loved us before, he would love us now. He would be with us to comfort and help us in a different way. How, I did not know. But I knew he would be with us—that I would not be alone.

I tried to analyze my emotions in an objective way. I did not feel that the death of the man I loved and the father of my children was a tragedy. My heart was filled with joy for him. I had a peace of mind that truly surpassed my human understanding. It was impossible to rationally understand how I could feel this way. It stayed with me night and day. It did not end. My imagination could not have had the power that this had over me. It was a very real thing. It did not falter. I seemed to have a compelling consciousness that expanded, exalted and far exceeded any experience I had ever known before, with an intense ellation that continued to overwhelm and envelope me with confidence, strength and insight.

I thanked God.

Day and night I thanked God for what I had been given.

My awareness of people and their problems seem to
have expanded; I would see people as never before. Where
everything had been muddled, it was now all bright and
clear, sharp and to the point. I felt surrounded by love and
goodness. I knew that love was the simple truth and
meaning of our existence—a beautiful, unselfish giving of
love to others. It seemed so very simple. It could solve the
problems of the world, if the world would listen.

I was extremely eager to share my joy and new
understanding with my friends. I wanted to release them
from the burden of worry over me. It was very difficult to
explain to people what had happened to me. How
impossible to describe a feeling or an emotion that another
has not felt. How to tell someone about love, when that
person has never felt it? How to explain music to the deaf
or the beauty of a rainbow to the blind? Everything I said
sounded absurd, irrational, totally inadequate to what was
happening to me. I wanted to say to everyone I knew and
saw, "Stop, stop, listen to me. I have something wonderful
to tell you. It happened to me, and it can happen to you
too. Please, please know there is something extra,
something beautiful and dynamic inside of us, waiting and
waiting for our needs and desire of it. Just ask! It's so
simple. Just ask and you shall receive."

The warm feeling of joy and peace free from
anxieties, tension, and worry remained with me.
Occasionally a flashback, a memory would cause a fleeting,
emptiness in me. I would recognize it and ask for help, and
I would feel pulled back up. How long could I keep this
up, I wondered? What kind of horror would I have if this

faith were to leave me now? I would be dashed to the depths of despair, after feeling the height of ecstasy. But two weeks went by and it persisted.

Slowly I was rearranging my household, getting back into a routine.

Handling the finances was a new role for me and a very demanding one right now. My health insurance was cancelled because it was with Mac's company. The first important thing I had to do would be to take out a new policy. A friend called and gave me the name of someone who knew the business well and would be glad to help me. I called up and arranged for an appointment.

That Monday afternoon I had started to sink a little. Not too badly, but I found that my confidence was beginning to ebb. Worries started to appear. I could not shake them. While they didn't engulf me, they were still there.

The insurance man came the next day. While we were talking business, he noticed my Edgar Cayce books. The books opened the door to a discussion of psychic phenomena. We talked about it for two hours. He told me that his child had died, and that he had communicated with his boy through the automatic writing of a friend. I was exhilarated! How exciting, I thought. "Could I possibly talk to this friend to see if she could communicate with Mac?" I asked.

"Sorry." he said. "She lives in California now." I was disappointed when he left. It would have been so thrilling to try to contact Mac.

My mind was whirling. If only I could find someone who could communicate with Mac. His last words to me had concerned the possibility of a life after death and I knew he would want to contact me now. But how? Good mediums were rare and many unscrupulous. I did not want to go that route. That left it up to me. It was very exciting to read about others communicating with the dead, but it was something else again to try it yourself. Venturing inward to another world scared me. It was full of fear and unknowns. Mac was there now though, and I wanted to share some of it with him. Slowly I began to realize that I should try to communicate with him myself. Try? I laughed. "Judy, you know you can do it." I knew that I could. I just knew that I had to.

I went to Ruth Montgomery's book* for advice and found the section on automatic writing. Let me see—"a prayerful meditation comes first . . . You should be well-rested . . . mornings worked best for her . . . a quiet, relaxed atmosphere was very important . . . you just hold your pen and relax . . . "

Wednesday morning I got up early to try out my pen. Very slowly, my hand began to move. I watched in amazement! My whole arm was moving as great circles were being drawn on the paper. The line was continuous as it flowed from one circle to another. The momentum was building up and the lines were getting darker and the circles larger. My whole arm seemed to separate from me,

*"A Search for Truth", New York, William Morrow & Co., 1967.

as if it were part of a machine. The pen was moving so fast now that it would occasionally fly off the paper. I ripped a sheet off the tablet. It was all I could do to hold the pen in my hand. Quickly the motion started again on the next sheet of paper. Frantic, beautiful circles, all in one continuous, flowing movement. I looked at my hand in disbelief. How could I possibly be doing this myself? I had always felt very inhibited and uncomfortable with a paint brush or sketching pencil in my hand. Creative expression in art was not my strong suit. The circles kept coming. The small paper I had was not large enough, and the pen would fly off the paper, wrinkling the edges with its attempt to get back on. I felt no control over my hand or my arm as the motion continued. I had about six pages of circles and this seemed to me to be enough for now. I said "I'm going to stop for now. I'll be back tomorrow morning." The pen began to slow down. Like a car running out of gas, it finally stopped. I looked at the clock in front of me. Four minutes had passed.

I called a friend of mine who had also read about automatic writing. I told her about my experience. "Don't you remember reading about the circles of joy?" she asked. "The spirit or guide is happy to be able to communicate with you, and this is its way of expressing it."

"O.K.," I said skeptically. "You draw a page of circles, and we will compare them." Later we laughed with glee at her row of small, shaky O's. Mine looked as though they had been drawn by a machine, a long continuous flow of circles.

I was exhilarated. I did have something here, and I knew it. I could hardly wait for morning to try again.

Kevin had read about automatic writing too, and he looked in astonishment at what I had done. "Mother," he said, "You could never have done this by yourself." He was right. I couldn't have.

I went through the same procedure again on Friday, only this time I decided to talk to it and see if I could get some information. How do you talk to a pen? The first thing is to be sure that no one is watching you. Lock your door—and close your draperies. My hand was on the paper now and, the circles began to form again. All right, I thought, Whoever you are, here's my message: I know Mac is happy. I felt strong pressure on my hand, and the lines became dark and firm. The motion and the intensity increased alarmingly. Instead of the circles, I began to get lines, back and forth. I felt a strong affirmation to what I had said. The pen never stopped moving; the circles came back again.

This time I said, "I know life is for giving and helping others." Back and forth it went again. Strong positive lines, back and forth, back and forth, back and forth. There was no question in my mind that my statement had been approved. It was time to finish. Four minutes had gone by, and I felt I should not devote too much to this. My world was here on earth, and I must live in it. "Goodbye" I said. "I'll be with you tomorrow morning." Slowly, the pen moved to a stop.

One of my friends had done some automatic writing, and I called her and told her what had happened. I expressed the fact that I felt I was close to writing because the lines were now becoming horizontal. I wondered who it was that was communicating with me? "My guide's name was John," she said. "He was killed in Viet Nam. The information that he gave me was not very important to me, so I stopped."

As I started writing the next morning the name John was impressed heavily on my mind—why I don't know—but to hope for a spirit whom I had known seemed to be asking too much. The gorgeous circles started coming again, and while I did enjoy them, I felt that enough was enough. It was time to get down to business.

"O.K., who are you?" I said. The pen began to move in shaky, wobbly lines. The word "Mother" came to my mind. I could not believe it until I opened my eyes and saw what I had written. Through the scrawley lines I was able to make out the letters M O T H E R . It was too much for me. Tears were streaming down my face and my body was trembling. I asked again and again, and the writing became clearer. It was easier to read. There was no question now. I was communicating with my mother. I asked questions: "Are you happy?" "Is Mac happy?" "Is this writing a good thing to do?" YES, YES, YES, was the answer I received. I was exhausted and overcome with joyous emotions. I said that I would quit for now but would be back tomorrow morning. The pen stopped.

Sunday I got up early to see what writing I could get before I took the children to church. I was well rested and eager for more explicit information. My pen started drawing circles again, but the circles seemed different.

They became smaller and smaller and then started to form letters. This was not like my mother's writing. "Who are you?" I asked. The word "Mac" came to my mind. I looked down to the paper and the letters had formed M A C through a continuous stream of circles. Again the tears flowed and my body throbbed with emotion. I asked again to be sure. And again. The circles kept making MAC, MAC. My pen didn't stop. I LOVE YOU TWEETIE, it said. I had to stop for a few minutes to calm myself, to wipe the tears from my eyes. "Are you happy?" I asked. YES, came the answer. The writing was more legible now. The circles had changed to zig zaggy lines, back and forth and close together. "Are the children all right?" I asked. YES came the reply. The writing was more clear. KEVIN WANTS TO LIVE. It wrote. "Will he?" I hurriedly asked. YES was the answer. The children were banging at my door. It was time to get ready for church. I had to stop for now. "I'll be with you tonight, tweetie," I said as I put away the pen.

I sat in church. Jimmy was crawling on me. Mary, was squirming, Mike and Kathleen were poking each other. Kevin was intent on what was going on around him. A typical Sunday, but oh, so different. My heart was teeming with happiness. My body pulsated with every beat of music. It was all I could do to keep from crying, tears of rejoicing. I looked at the faces around me. A University chapel draws a mixed bag of people, a blend of many colors and interesting types. Today they all seemed to radiate the splendor of God. The light of love was all

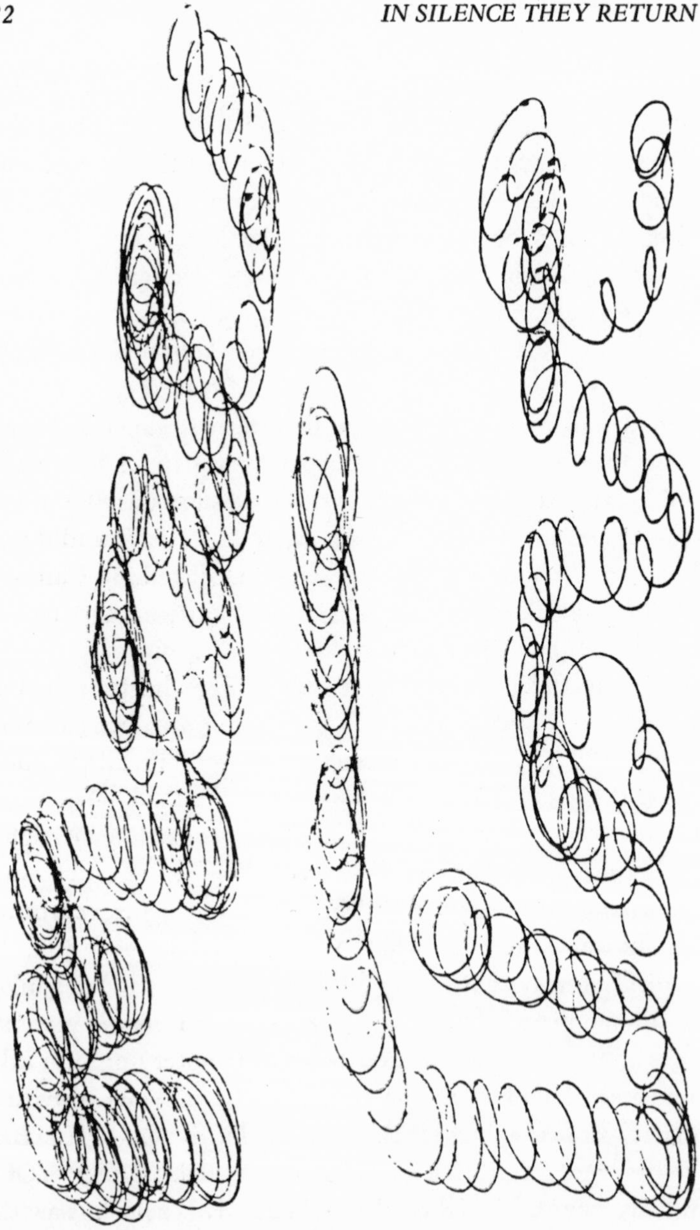

around me. Thank God! was all I could pray. Home to the unmade beds, mouths to feed, dirty dishes, and an unkempt house.

"Mom, can Carol stay for dinner?"

"Sure," I replied.

"How about Tommy?"

"O.K." I said. One more wouldn't make any difference at that point.

It was a busy day! My mind was not on what I was doing. All I could think about was what I had written. I thought I must be going out of my mind. How could I really believe this? I felt it was true, but my mind told me I was crazy. I laughed at myself. The next thing I know, I'll be sitting in a corner of a mental institution, tearing up little pieces of paper covered with circles.

Our dinner guests had gone. I was tired. I thought I'd go to bed early. The children were in the living room, watching their favorite Sunday night program. Kevin said, "Mom, I have to draw an example of an optical illusion for school tomorrow." I told him to get started on it right away and to use the encyclopedia for help. I said I was going to try some more writing. I went into the bedroom and closed the door.

My circles came in again, only this time they went right into letters. I LOVE YOU, they wrote. I did not ask any questions, but instead let my pen go. YOU WOULD LIKE IT HERE. NO ONE IS UNHAPPY—YOU WILL BE VERY HAPPY HERE. I went on. I WILL HELP YOU WITH HOME WORK. "You? You will help me with

homework?" I said. YES, was my answer. "Oh, come on now Mac. This is too much. You never wanted to help with homework when you were here, why now? This is ridiculous! Let's try it again." I WILL HELP YOU WITH HOMEWORK. "You really mean that you want to help Kevin with his homework?" YES, was my answer. "You want to work with Kevin by yourself?" YES, came again. I shrugged my shoulders and mumbled. "This should be interesting." I went in the dining room and said, "Kevin, your father wants to help you with your homework."

"What?" he asked.

"Your father wrote and said he wants to help you with your homework."

"But Mom—I don't know what it's all about."

"Kev, just sit down at the table with your pen and paper and see what happens."

Kevin gave me a strange look, but sat down. I went back into my bedroom. Ten minutes had passed when Kevin came into my room. "Mom, I get some yes and no answers to questions I ask but nothing else. I have to get my homework done."

"All right," Kev, "I'll see what I can do." "Mac," I said, "What shall we do?" I put my pen down on the paper again. In clear, zigzagging lettering came the words *BOOK OF KNOWLEDGE*. *"Book of Knowledge?"* I laughed. "That's not right." The writing continued. EVERYONE IS BOTHERING ME.

The T.V. was blaring. The children were all up running around. "Would you like me to put them to bed?" YES, was my answer. "Then would you like to work with

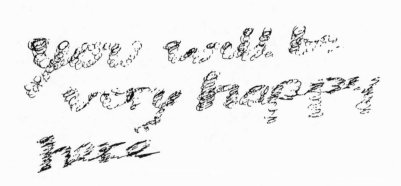

Kevin?" YES, again. MOTHER STAY AWAY, it wrote. I put the children to bed, turned off the T.V. and told Kevin to try again. After fifteen frustrating minutes with no luck, he called me. I went into the dining room, took out my pen to see what I would get. *BOOK OF KNOWLEDGE* STAY AWAY FROM KEVIN. "Kev," I said, "Daddy wants to work with you alone. If I'm near you, he can't do it. Please try again." Kevin tried again, this time for half an hour, but he was not able to receive anything. He came to me once more. "Mom, will you please try again?"

"All right," I said. So I started writing again. *BOOK OF KNOWLEDGE*. This was really becoming absurd. "We don't even have the *Book of Knowledge*. You've made a mistake," I chuckled. "We have the *World Book*. Remember when I talked you into buying it? You must have forgotten the name." The pen was moving again. YOU DO NOT HAVE THE BOOK. CALLAHANS. The Callahans were our next door neighbors. This was getting to be exciting! I called their house. I asked Marilyn if they had this set of encyclopedias. "Yes," she replied, "we have a very old set in a box in the basement. You may borrow it if you like." I thanked her and went back to my writing. My pen wrote out PAGE 3313 BOOK NUMBER 10. I sent Kevin over to the Callahans to borrow the book. We were very confused and disappointed. Page 3313 did not have anything to do with optical illusion. It was the story of Thomas Carlyle. By this time Kevin and I were both very tired. There seemed to be something to this, but what, I didn't know. Meanwhile Kevin had to do his homework and get to bed. I mentioned this out loud. My pen came

back with the reply   HE WILL DO IT NOW I LOVE
YOU   I LOVE YOU

My mind was whirling with confusion. Kevin did his
homework, and we both went to bed. After that
experience we both needed a good night's sleep.

I awoke the next morning, refreshed and ready to
solve the puzzle. The *Book of Knowledge* was beside my
bed. I picked it up and turned to page 3313, the story of
Thomas Carlyle. I began to read Carlyle's life story:

... from both parents the boy learned that duty and service to
God are important. He knew that a man must follow his own
conscience. When Carlyle was in college, he read a book of essays
by David Hume, and Edward Gibbon's great history about the fall
of the Roman Empire. For a long time these books made him
very unhappy because they made him doubt that religious faith
of his childhood. All that he had valued before seemed worthless.
When he went back to Edinburgh a few years later, he was so
depressed that life seemed hardly worthwhile.

But one day he felt a new kind of faith and courage surging
into his spirit. He was like a runner who suddenly gets his second
wind, and leaps forward, refreshed, to win a race. Henceforth,
Carlyle although by nature gloomy, and often sick and weary,
never doubted the truth of his ideals. This change of heart led
him to write the books that made him great. Here is an example
from his important book, SARTOR RESARTIS:

" ... often (he wrote) when I read of formal occasions,
coronations, Royal Drawing Rooms, receptions and so, how Duke
this is presented by Archduke that, and Colonel A by General B,
and unnumerable Bishops, Admirals and other Big wigs are
introduced, then I try to imagine what this solemn scene would
be like if, on a sudden, as by some enchanted wand, the Clothes
should fly off the whole crowd; And Dukes, Grandees, Bishops,

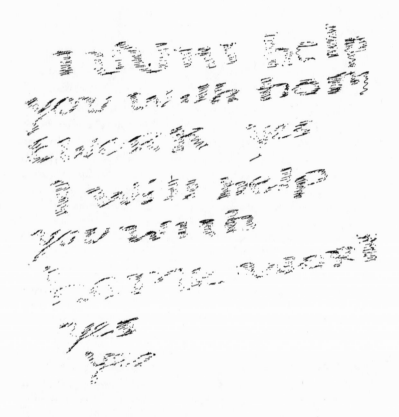

Generals, the annointed King himself, every mother's son of them, stand straddling there, not a shirt on them; and I know not whether to laugh or weep!''
This is a rather amusing picture of course, but Carlyle meant to be more than amusing. He was trying to say that most men and women dress up the truth in so many garments that you often cannot recognize it. Just as customs and habits and pretending and little fibs cover up reality. We must get rid of the pretenses and the lies, he insisted, if we are to get at the truth of things.''

So! This was Kevin's homework. This was the message for Kevin from his father. The philosophy was so like Mac, with his firm conviction that he must follow his own conscience. Carlyle's depression was like Mac's also. It was very significant that Kevin (who is a ski racer) would know what it was like to grab for the second wind. As Mac had learned to mentally strip the color from people's skin and remove the prejudice, Carlyle wondered what it would be like to strip the clothes off the pompous and illuminate the pretense and lies.

The enormity of what I read overwhelmed me. I took out my pen and paper and started to write. Mac signed in, in his zigzag signature. Am I right, Mac? I asked. YES I AM GOING TO HELP KEVIN SO HE CAN HELP THE WORLD. YOU ARE GOING TO HELP TOO! WE WILL STILL WORK TOGETHER—BETTER THAN BEFORE—TRUST IN ME—I KNOW THE ANSWERS NOW—I WILL GUIDE YOU THRU BOOKS. I WILL PROVIDE YOUR ANSWERS FOR YOU. YOU KNOW THE ANSWERS YOURSELF BUT I WILL HELP YOU TOO. LIFE IS BEAUTIFUL BUT NOT AS NICE AS

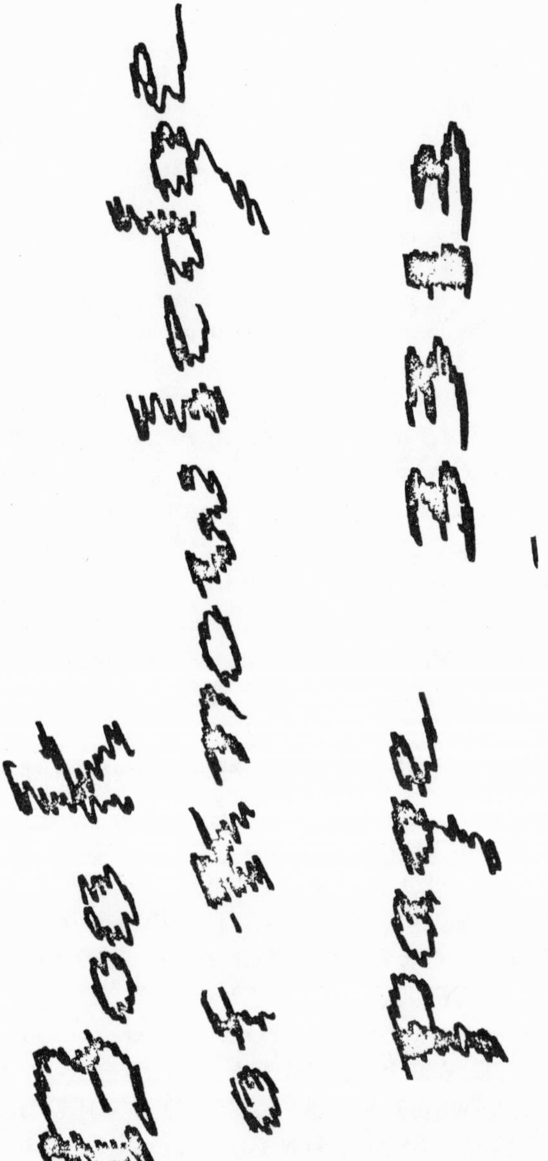
Book
of Knowledge
Page 33.

THIS—YOUR WORLD IS FILLED WITH SO MUCH
HATE. I WILL BE WITH YOU ALWAYS. "How are the
children?" I asked. MICHAEL MISSES ME—GIVE HIM
MORE LOVE—KATHLEEN WILL BE ALL RIGHT—SHE
IS LIKE YOU—MARY SUSAN IS FINE NOW TOO.
KEVIN HAS MUCH TO LIVE FOR—JIMMY IS
ALREADY THERE—NO JIMMY WILL NOT DIE BUT
JIMMY KNOWS WHAT I KNOW—CHILDREN ARE NOT
SO INNOCENT—THEY UNDERSTAND MORE THAN
WE GIVE THEM CREDIT FOR—DON'T
UNDERESTIMATE CHILDREN THEY KNOW LOVE
AND THEY WILL LEARN TO GIVE IT—DON'T KNOW
WHAT ELSE TO SAY NOW I HAVE MORE TO LEARN
ALSO WE SHALL LEARN TOGETHER.—I LOVE
YOU I LOVE YOU

"Thank you Mac," I said. "Not only have you given
me a meaningful philosophy for our children to be raised
with, but you have left me with proof of your existence."

yes
yes

you do not have

page 33 13 have you the book

do not have callahan?

the book yes

yes

Book number 111 no 10

A Movie Called Life

My days were busy.

There were many new demands for my time. Before Mac had died, my role was basically domestic. I was a housewife. Now I was a widow. At 33 years of age, the responsibilities that were ahead for me could have oppressed me. Instead, I was stimulated by the challenge. I knew that it would take everything I had to fill the ambiguous state that I was in. Society had little to say about the role of the widow at my age. I was too old to be a swinging single and too young for a weeping widow. I would have to find the way myself.

The world of business was the first new door that I had to open. It could not be put off, because the insurance had to be taken care of, bank accounts changed, social security applications filled out, the safety deposit box inventoried, and investments made. There were forms to fill out and dates to give. Sign your name here. Sign there. It went on and on and on. Before, my daily routine involved with children and neighbors; now I was meeting with lawyers, bankers, insurance men, brokers, and investment analysts. Yes, my role had changed. And I was tired. Very tired. I would collapse in bed early every night, and before falling into an exhausted sleep, I would take out my pad of paper and pen to write.

I spent a few minutes in silent prayer and meditation before beginning. Mac would usually sign in, in his now familiar zigzag signature. But sometimes it would be my mother who wrote: MAC IS BUSY NOW. She said one day. HE HAS MANY THINGS TO DO AND TO LEARN. HE WANTS TO HELP YOU VERY MUCH AND IS DOING MANY THINGS FOR YOU. HE FELT BAD ABOUT LEAVING YOU. She would give me the same advice and comfort that she did in life. Always encouraging, she told me not to worry, that I would have much help.

The writing was very legible now. It had progressed to a handwriting similar but different from my own. The messages usually came to my mind first, and then my hand wrote them out hurriedly. There were times when I did not know what was coming, and then the writing would be in zigzag lines or in circles. Sometimes it would be hard to get a word and I would have to try many times. I would deliberately blank my mind to let the answer come through it. LET ME SAY IT, they would write. Apparently my thought process had interfered. I would then detach my mind and let my hand get the answer.

When the writing stopped, it was as though a big white door had been closed in my face. There was nothing more. That was it. My mind was a blank again. So little was the writing a part of me that I could not recall what I had written. I had to read it over. When they had something to tell me, it would come fast—so fast that I could hardly write quickly enough. I would have three or four pages in a few minutes. It seemed to just flow out of me.

Mother and Mac were both concerned about my health. They wanted me to get plenty of rest and more sleep. They were right, I knew, but I became a little irritated by their always telling me. "It's all right for you," I thought, "You don't have to worry about sleep or about doing all of the things I have to do." DON'T WORRY, THEY'LL GET DONE, they'd answer. Of course, things did get done, and I began to worry less about them.

One night, I went over to the University of Minnesota to hear a speaker. I was home by 11 o'clock. As I started to write, I received a scolding from Mac. WHY DON'T YOU STAY HOME MORE OFTEN. That really made me mad. "You, you of all people telling me to stay home! You! who were hardly ever home!"

The writing went on—YOU'RE TIRED AND THE CHILDREN MISSED YOU AND WANTED YOU HOME. I hadn't been out very much—maybe twice a week at night. I didn't want to be a recluse and knew that I needed adult conversation. I didn't feel guilty about this. "O.K. Mac," I said. "What happened while I was gone?" MARY WOULDN'T GO TO BED AND JIMMY MISSED YOU. I called to Kevin. "Kevin, what happened while I was not at home?"

"Well, Mary would not go to bed," he said "and Jimmy wanted to sleep in your bed. I guess he was lonesome for you." All I could do was to laugh. To think that Mac was home baby-sitting while I was out. It was too much. I chuckled to myself thinking of how things had changed.

The next morning I had a talk with the children. They understood about my writing and the experience that I was having. They accepted it as I did. My thoughts went back to what the Catholic church had taught me about guardian angels. How well I remembered hearing in my religion class that we all had a guardian angel who watched over us and would protect and help us in time of need. I told the children that their father had been with them last night, and I repeated what he had written to me. Their eyes opened wide and they agreed that he was right about what had happened with Mary and Jimmy. I reminded them that they would never be alone. There would always be some good spirit to help them. If it wasn't their father, it would be their grandmother or someone else. The tears came to my eyes when Michael said, "We are so lucky to have a dad that loves us and wants to help us." If only we all had the beautiful faith of children, I thought, our world would be so much happier. Mary came to me with a picture of an angel with the words under it—Guardian Angel. "Is this what daddy looks like?" she asked. Picturing Mac with large, fluffy, voluminous, white wings flapping in the wind made me laugh. "No, sweetheart," I said, "daddy doesn't look like that." That was the one thing I was sure of. "But don't forget, even though we can't see daddy, he is often with us to help us when we need him. Remember too, that he can tell me things that you are doing, so let's not have any more problems when I am gone." That was something they hadn't considered. They would really have to be careful now. Guardian angels would be a disadvantage at times.

The checks from Mac's life insurance had arrived. Although it seemed like a lot of money, I knew that it would have to be invested well in order to provide an income for the six of us for many years. The expensive years were still ahead of me with Kevin nearing his teens not to mention college years in the future. My thoughts about the stock market had been optimistic lately. I had been telling Mac all summer that we were on the bottom and that it would pick up in the fall. I thought to myself that now should be a good time to invest. Stocks should be at a good low. I had friends in the banking and investment business who could give me good advice. I was eager to get the money situation settled and an income coming in.

I had an appointment one morning at 11 o'clock to meet my banker and an investment analyst at the bank to discuss how the money should be invested. I was busy getting ready to take Jimmy to a friend's house and doing the usual morning household chores when a thought came to my mind. Maybe I should do some automatic writing. Even though I was in a hurry, I took my pen and paper and began to write. Mac signed in. BUY HI YIELD BONDS. DON'T INVEST MARKET VERY SHAKY. I

a

LOVE YOU TWEETIE. "Thank you," I said and laughed. "It looks as if you're still in the investment business, Mac."

As I walked into the bank building, I felt ten feet tall and brimming with self-confidence. It was the first time I had been to the bank; yet I felt as relaxed and familiar, as if it was my neighborhood supermarket. The atmosphere was conservative, reserved. The men were very solicitous, figuratively bending over backwards to make everything as easy to understand as possible. I chuckled to myself—"It's the typical widow's treatment, and they're doing a good job. Little do they know what I know."

"Now, Judy," one said, "here are the stocks that we advise you to invest in." The other handed me a sheet of paper with everything listed on it. I studied it carefully. Yes, I thought, they had done a good job. It was what Mac would have called a "widow's portfolio." It was diverse. The yield would be good. The risk low. It allowed for growth potential. I was familiar with the stocks on the list and discussed them. "Yes," I concluded, "you have done a good job. These stocks would be good to buy——sometime. But not now." I felt confidence surging within me as I went on. "Now is not a good time to get into the market. It is very shaky and will be for quite some time. It definitely would not be a good time to invest. What I would like to do now would be to put my money in some high yield bonds. The interest rates are high, and it would be smart to take advantage of them. They might possibly go higher. The timing is right to get into bonds now, and I want to capitalize on them."

There was silence. "Well, aaah, yes that might be a good idea. In fact, it sounds like a very good idea." The men looked a little uncomfortable. Their manner suggested that this was a very unusual widow.

I saw my banker at a party a few months later. "Say, Judy, you sure were smart to put your money in bonds. The market has gone down appreciably. You would have lost quite a bit of money if you had invested in stocks. But, putting it into bonds you did very well." "Thank you, Mac." I said to myself. I looked at the paper the next morning. The financial page had nothing but woe for the stock market conditions. "More money is pouring into the bond market now as the stocks steadily decline," I read. Of course I thought. Of course. Mac was right. There was no doubt in my mind that he wouldn't be.

Before he died, Mac had the feeling that the market would be doing better by fall. Yet, he who spent most of his time selling stocks was now telling me to buy bonds. This advice had turned out to be very wise. How did he know more about finance now then he did when he was alive? I was confused.

The next night I did some writing before I went to sleep. It had been a busy day. There were so many things to do. Even though I thrived on activity and responsibility, it seemed I could never get ahead of my obligations. DON'T WORRY TWEETIE, Mac wrote, I CAN SEE EVERYTHING THAT'S GOING TO HAPPEN TO YOU. ALL OF YOUR PROBLEMS ARE OVER FOR YOU NOW. I WILL HELP YOU. BELIEVE

ME. YOU'VE GOT IT MADE! I KNOW EVERYTHING
THAT'S GOING TO HAPPEN TO YOU.

"I know everything that's going to happen to you." I
went to sleep with that thought in my mind. The next
morning I awoke with the question, How? How do you
know everything that's going to happen to me? I began to
write, ITS BECAUSE OF TIME TWEETIE. Mac
wrote. TIME IS A CONCEPT THAT IS DIFFICULT TO
DEFINE IN OUR WORLD. IT DOES NOT
EXIST. OUR WORLD IS OPEN TO
EVERYTHING. YOURS IS SO VERY
LIMITED. YOUR WORLD IS LIKE LIVING IN A
SMALL BOX. YOU CAN SEE SO LITTLE. OURS IS
OPEN TO EVERYTHING. I CAN SEE YOUR PAST
NOW AND, FUTURE IN A GLANCE. WE SEE THE
WHOLE WIDE PICTURE HERE. IT IS SO
BEAUTIFUL. THIS IS WHY I HAVE SO MUCH TO
TELL YOU. IT IS DIFFICULT FOR ME TO BE
SPECIFIC ABOUT DATES. DATES DON'T MEAN
ANYTHING HERE, I USUALLY HAVE TO MAKE A
CALCULATED GUESS. BUT I CAN SEE WHAT IS
GOING TO HAPPEN.

I put my pen down and read and reread many times
what I had just written. I laughed. "You stinker," I
mumbled, "you're really one up on me now. To think that
you are really able to know everything that's going to
happen to me."

Time. What a very limited understanding we have of
it in our earthly life, I thought. It is difficult for us to

remember the past. Sometimes we even forget what we did yesterday. A day, a month, a year ago was all in the past to be shelved away with the rest of our soon-to-be-forgotten memories.

Today is where we live. Today, the now, this very moment, is what we have been given to make more meaningful and helpful to others. Today will soon be gone and become a part of our past.

The future we could plan and dream about, but as I well knew, dreams could be destroyed in an instant—in a flash, like the skid of a car as it careens into another and destroys the life within.

Many times tiny glimpses could be seen through a crack in the door of the future. It had been opened to me with the premonitions of my mother's and Mac's deaths. It is given to many of us in the form of dreams, intuition, and feelings. Now, the door could be opened further for me through my communications with Mac. The possiblities that this presented in helping other people excited me. I considered life a process of learning and growing. The experiences that we endure are a part of this development. Much of our unhappiness could be avoided by going in the right direction. Perhaps Mac could help me to help others by utilizing his ability to see the future. I began to ask him. "What can I do for——?" I mentioned the names of friends who were having problems. PRAY FOR HER—PRAY FOR HIM, was the answer I got. Pray. That was interesting. In Mac's lifetime, he had helped other people through his own resources, but he hadn't used prayer for a long time. But now in almost every

communication that I received from him I was told to pray
for someone.

I believed in prayer. It seemed to help me through so
many tough situations in the last few years. It had become
an increasingly important part of my life. I felt that it had
worked for me. Prayer had given me so much extra
strength and help that I needed. But now I wanted to
know how prayer works. It was like looking at a clock. I
could see the hands going round and round. I knew that
the clock was showing me the correct time, but I wanted
to take off the cover and examine it. I wanted to take this
word prayer and open it up and see how it worked.

With pen and paper in hand, I asked Mac to help me
solve this question. EVERYTHING THAT HAPPENS TO
YOU ON THIS EARTH IS THE RESULT OF YOUR
FREE WILL NOW. WHEN YOU USE GOD YOU WILL
BE GUIDED BY HIM—YOU ARE THE ONE WHO
MAKES YOUR EARTH LEVEL, WITH OR WITHOUT
GOD—DEPENDING ON *YOUR* CHOICE. TO CHOOSE
OR NOT TO CHOOSE GOD MAKES THE
DIFFERENCE. THIS IS WHERE PRAYER COMES
IN—IT IS DIRECT COMMUNICATION WITH
GOD. ASK FOR HIS HELP. HE WANTS
THIS—NOTHING IS TOO BIG FOR HIM. WHAT HE
WANTS IS FOR YOU TO BELIEVE IN HIM. PRAYERS
ARE ANSWERED BY GOD THROUGH SPIRITS SUCH
AS MYSELF. NOW TO PRAY TO THE SAINTS IS ALL
WELL AND GOOD. BUT REMEMBER, WE ARE ALL
SO-CALLED SAINTS ON MY LEVEL AND WE CAN
ALL DO DIFFERENT THINGS, DEPENDING ON OUR

OWN TALENTS. I AM A SAINT TOO! BELIEVE ME, THERE ARE A LOT OF THINGS THAT I CAN DO HERE THAT MANY SPIRITS CAN'T DO. MY GREATEST ABILITY IS TO WORK THRU PEOPLE. THERE ARE MANY "TRICKS" I COULD DO IF I WANTED TO WORK HARD. I MIGHT LATER, BUT MY "THING" IS TO WORK THRU PEOPLE. IT'S ALL A MATTER OF KNOWING YOURSELF, JUST LIKE ON YOUR LEVEL! TO HELP PEOPLE JUST PRAY. PRAY HARD FOR THEM AND THEN STAY OPEN AND SLOWLY YOU WILL SEE THINGS HAPPEN. KEEP PRAYING AND YOU WILL FIND WHAT ELSE YOU CAN DO. PRAYER IS THE FIRST. IT'S LIKE PUTTING THE KEY IN THE IGNITION TO START THE CAR. THE CAR WON'T START UNTIL YOU DO, AND IT WON'T KEEP MOVING IF ITS TURNED OFF. DON'T FORGET TOO THAT PRAYER IS ANSWERED IN GOD'S TIME AND NOT IN YOURS. A PRAYER IS NEVER LOST. IT WILL BE ANSWERED WHEN IT IS BEST FOR YOU AND HOW IT WILL BE BEST FOR YOU.

What a beautiful answer I had been given. The analogy between starting the car and praying is such an earthly and masculine approach. How like Mac who loved to tinker with his car.

I thought all day about what had been written to me. That night I started writing again. This time it was my mother's signature, which came through. DON'T FORGET TO THANK GOD FOR WHAT YOU HAVE

RECEIVED. IT IS JUST LIKE THANKING FOR A
PRESENT YOU RECEIVE ON EARTH. YOU WOULD
ALWAYS THANK SOMEONE FOR A GIFT THAT YOU
RECEIVED. IT IS THE SAME WITH PRAYER. YOU
SHOULD NOT FORGET TO THANK GOD.

"Yes Mother," I said, "I won't forget." I felt like a
small child again with mother reminding me about proper
etiquette.

As the days passed, I began to see how Mac was able
to work through people, as he said he could. Kevin was in
need of new ski boots. They were expensive, but very
important for racing that meant so much to him. I felt
strongly that he should continue the sport. Racing was
very difficult. It demanded a lot of time, money, and hard
work, but it could teach great lessons in self-control and
perseverance. It would be difficult for me to handle all of
the expense and work involved this year, but I didn't
worry. Help seemed to come from everywhere.

But Kevin needed his boots now. They were
something that couldn't be put off. They had to be
ordered, and this took time. He was after me to get going
on it. One night, while I was writing, Mac wrote, DON'T
BUY KEVIN HIS SKI BOOTS. I WILL GET THEM FOR
YOU. THIS IS IMPORTANT. HE HAS TO TRUST IN
ME. I WILL GET THEM FOR HIM. I showed the
message to Kevin. "Oh, mom, really. What's he going to
do, drop them from the sky? I need those boots."

"I don't know how its going to be done, Kev, but
someone will probably call to say that they will buy you

the boots. He said he will take care of it, and he will." I really had talked myself out on a limb. I desperately wanted Kevin to trust in Mac and to believe in him. It was very important. If someone didn't come through with an offer to buy him the boots then he and I both would be disappointed and disillusioned. Every time the phone rang, I thought, "Well maybe, this is it." But it wasn't. One day, I stopped by to see my friend and neighbor, Mary. We were eating a sandwich when her husband, Reyn, walked in. "Say, Judy, I would like to buy Kevin some ski equipment. What does he need?" Reyn asked.

I shrieked with joy, "So you're the one!" I told them both the story of what Mac had written.

"I don't know if I am the one Mac picked out, but I'll be happy to get the boots for Kev," he said. He did.

The messages I received from Mac and Mother were always helpful. They comforted me when I felt dejected and encouraged me when I needed the boost. Often when I heard the siren of an ambulance or read about a death, my mind would be plagued by scenes from Mac's accident with his mutilated body contorting in agony. The vision of rescuers trying to pull the collapsed steering wheel from his sunken chest while blood rushed from the gash on his head would overwhelm me and I would hurt and be numb with helplessness again. One night I had been bothered by those thoughts for hours. Finally, I took up my paper and pen and started to write.

TWEETIE, Mac wrote, THE ACCIDENT WAS HARDER ON YOU THAN ME, BELIEVE ME! AT

FIRST IT WAS LIKE BEING RIPPED APART, SOON
EVERYTHING WAS BLACK WITH INTENSE
HEAT — THEN A GRADUAL DRIFTING,
DRIFTING––DRIFTING AWAY, A FLOATING, THEN
I SEEMED TO BE LOOKING DOWN–DOWN UPON THE
ACCIDENT SCENE. IT WAS VERY STRANGE BUT I
FELT SO BADLY FOR MYSELF. IT WAS JUST LIKE I
WAS WATCHING MYSELF, BUT THE MYSELF I WAS
WATCHING WAS ANOTHER PERSON. SOON THERE
WERE OTHERS AROUND TALKING TO ME, HELPING
ME, BUT IT WASN'T TILL I SAW YOUR MOTHER, SHE
SAID, "MAC, MAC, ITS FLORENCE, I CAME TO BE
WITH YOU" THAT I REALIZED I WAS DEAD. I FELT
SO BADLY, BUT I WAS SO CONFUSED. I DIDN'T
LEAVE YOU BUT STAYED CLOSE TO YOU. WHEN
YOU FELT BETTER THEY SAID I SHOULD LEAVE SO
I COULD LEARN. IT IS LIKE A NEW BEGINNING
AND MY ONLY REGRETS ARE YOU AND THE
CHILDREN, THEY ARE TOO YOUNG FOR THAT BUT
THEY LEARNED AND SO DID WE ALL. AND NOW I
AM ON THE OTHER SIDE, WATCHING, LISTENING,
HEARING AND THINKING EVERYONES' THOUGHTS,
BUT SO UNABLE TO PARTICIPATE. SOMETIMES I
FEEL LIKE I'M WATCHING A MOVIE–LETS CALL IT
LIFE! HOWEVER, MY ONE REAL CHANCE IS IN YOU
BECAUSE IT IS YOU THAT I AM ABLE TO REALLY
REACH. I AM ABLE TO GET THROUGH TO OTHERS
SOMETIMES AND IT IS FUN WHEN SOMEONE ALL
OF A SUDDEN COMES UP WITH AN IDEA THAT I
HAVE INSPIRED. THE OLD LIGHT BULB IN THE

HEAD—THATS ME! I AM FAIRLY WELL ADJUSTED TO THOSE ON THIS PLANE, HOWEVER, SO MANY HERE HAVE HANGUPS LIKE MINE. I GUESS WE ALL HERE HAVE PROBLEMS WE HAVE TO WORK OUT. MAYBE THATS WHY THE CHURCH CALLS IT PURGATORY. I KNOW THERE ARE BETTER LEVELS OF CONSCIOUSNESS THAN WHERE I AM BUT I'M NOT READY YET. AS I RECALL THE CHURCH AND ITS PRAYING FOR THOSE IN PURGATORY—THEY WERE RIGHT. WE DO NEED HELP, BUT NO MORE THAN WE DID IN THE LEVEL CALLED LIFE. WE ALL SEEM TO BE ABLE TO PUT OURSELVES THROUGH WHAT WE DESERVE. FORTUNATELY HERE THERE IS NOTHING TO HIDE BEHIND AND WE MUST FACE OURSELVES AS WE REALLY ARE. OUR WORLD IS SO DIFFERENT THAN YOURS AND I AM DEALING WITH MORE ABSOLUTES NOW. Absolutes? my mind questioned this. O.K., LET ME EXPLAIN. ABSOLUTES LIKE LOVE—A PERFECT GIVING LOVE AND HOW TO ACHIEVE THIS. PATIENCE—FOR THE UNDERSTANDING OF EVERYONES' DIFFERENCES AND RESPECT OF EVERY INDIVIDUAL FOR HIMSELF. KINDNESS TO ALL. GENTLENESS, AND MOST OF ALL HELPING OTHERS. THIS IS SO IMPORTANT—TO HELP OTHERS. WE ARE ABLE TO DO THIS IN MANY WAYS. YOU WILL BE SURPRISED WHEN YOU BECOME A SPIRIT AT THE VAST WAYS THAT HUMANS ARE HELPED BY SPIRITS. THANK YOU

FOR LETTING ME EXPRESS MYSELF. YOU HAVE
THE UPPER HAND NOW—AND IT IS YOUR HAND I
APPRECIATE SO MUCH. I LOVE YOU.

One night, I felt especially rested and decided to go
to my room early and just see what came from my pen. I
had no questions to ask. I merely wanted to let the spirit
speak. It was Mac who signed in. I LOVE YOU
TWEETIE.
LOVE IS THE ANSWER. IT IS THE ONLY
ANSWER. IT IS THE ONLY THING THAT IS
REAL. IT IS ENORMOUS. IT IS GOD. GOD IS THE
ULTIMATE LOVE. HE IS ALL LOVE, AND THRU
LOVE WE FIND GOD. IT IS THRU AND WITH LOVE
THAT WE SOAR AND CLIMB. IT IS OUR LOVE FOR
GOD AND OUR RECOGNIZING GOD IN OTHER
PEOPLE AND THRU USING THE GOD IN US THAT WE
REACH THE ULTIMATE GOD. IF ONLY MORE
PEOPLE WOULD KNOW TRUE LOVE. LOVE IS THE
ANSWER. IT IS A BOND THAT DOES NOT DIE.
OUR PROBLEMS AND THE STUMBLING WE GO
THROUGH IS OUR SELFISH LOVE OF OUR
HUMANESS, NOT OUR GODLINESS. FOR WITH OUR
HUMANESS ALONE WE ARE NOTHING. KEEP
REMEMBERING; YOU AS A PHYSICAL BEING ALONE
ARE NOTHING, BUT THE COMPLETE YOU, THE GOD
IN YOU, IS EVERYTHING. THE BODY IS
NOTHING. IT IS THE SOUL THAT MATTERS. THAT
IS THE GOD IN YOU. THERE ARE THREE LEVELS
OF CONSCIOUSNESS: THE CONSCIOUS, THE

SUB-CONSCIOUS, AND THE GOD LEVEL. GOD HAD GIVEN YOU WARNINGS OF MY DEATH–OR PHYSICALLY LEAVING YOU. I DON'T LIKE THE WORD DEATH. THIS WAS TO PREPARE YOUR CONSCIOUS MIND SO IT WOULD ACCEPT IT BETTER. IT DID! IT WAS A BEAUTIFUL ACCEPTANCE OF WHAT HAPPENED. IF YOUR CONSCIOUS MIND ALONE HAD TO ACCEPT THIS, IT WOULD LEAVE YOU FULL OF DESPAIR, BITTERNESS AND ANGER. THOSE FEELINGS ARE NOT IN YOU. YOU ONLY FEEL LOVE FOR GOD, FOR ME, AND THOSE AROUND YOU. YOU ARE THE BEST TESTIMONY OF AN AFTERLIFE.

THE REASON I AM WITH YOU IS BECAUSE OF MY LOVE FOR YOU. I KNOW YOU NEED ME, AND I KNOW I CAN HELP YOU. YOUR GOALS ARE HIGH, AND BY HELPING YOU I CAN HELP MYSELF TOO! IF YOU WANTED ME JUST FOR YOURSELF I WOULD HAVE TO LEAVE YOU, AS THIS WOULD HARM BOTH OF US. SELFISHNESS I COULD NOT ENCOURAGE. BUT YOU ASKED TO BE USED TO HELP OTHERS, AND THIS IS BEAUTIFUL. SO BY HELPING YOU TO DO THIS, I HELP MYSELF.

KEEP WRITING LIKE THIS. BIT, BY BIT MORE THINGS WILL COME OUT THAT YOU CAN SORT OUT LATER. I WILL DEAL WITH MANY CONCEPTS, BUT LOVE IS THE BASIS. IT IS SO SIMPLE–IT COULD BE WRITTEN IN SO FEW WORDS.

THIS IS ENOUGH FOR NOW. I LOVE YOU. I LOVE YOU.

As I read over what I had written that evening, I glanced at a picture that a friend had given me. It was of Mac, taken shortly before his death on a warm, Sunday afternoon. There was laughter, song, and gaiety in the air that day. Everyone was happy. The memory came back to me clearly. I could see Mac sitting on a lawn chair, with his guitar in his hands and his ever-present pipe by his side. Beads of water still clung to his chest from his swim in the lake. His hair curled softly around his face as on a child. His face was deeply tanned. He looked relaxed, contented. My eyes became misty as I thought of him. I loved him. Mac was never more. As the tears rolled down my face, I took my pencil and wrote. It was Mac. WHEN YOU THINK OF ME, THINK OF ME AS I AM NOW. THIS IS SO MUCH MORE BEAUTIFUL THAN THE PAST. I HAD SO MANY PROBLEMS THEN. I DON'T HAVE THEM ANYMORE. I WILL MAKE YOU HAPPY. I CAN DO SO MUCH MORE FOR YOU THAN I COULD DO BEFORE. BELIEVE ME, THERE ARE SO MANY SOULS THAT WOULD LIKE TO HAVE THE COMMUNICATION THAT WE HAVE NOW. WE ARE SO LUCKY TO HAVE THIS. IT IS VERY BEAUTIFUL. DON'T FORGET––I WILL HELP YOU, I WILL ALWAYS HELP YOU. YOU'RE NOT ALONE, TWEETIE. YOU WILL BE SO HAPPY NOW. YOU KNOW YOU HAVE GOD WITH YOU, AND THERE IS MORE OF GOD IN ME AND YOUR MOTHER TO HELP YOU. YOU GAVE US MUCH, AND WE WILL SHARE WITH YOU WHAT WE HAVE. LOVE IS SHARING. LOVE NEVER STOPS. IT GROWS AND

GROWS. YOU WILL LOVE MORE AND MORE AND SEE LOVE IN EVERYBODY. IT IS THERE. REMEMBER GOD IS WITH US AND ALL WE HAVE TO DO IS DESIRE HIM. HE WILL BE OURS TO GUIDE US THRU LIFE AND IT WILL BE BEAUTIFUL. YOU ARE SO FORTUNATE TO KNOW ALL OF THIS NOW. YOUR PATH WILL BE SO MUCH EASIER. YOUR RESPONSIBILITIES WILL BE GREAT BUT YOU WILL BE ABLE TO ACHIEVE MUCH. YOU WILL KNOW GREAT HAPPINESS FROM THIS. LIFE IS FULFILLMENT WITH GOD. YOU HAVE THIS AND YOUR PATH WILL BE SO EASY NOW.

TEACH THE CHILDREN HOW TO GIVE LOVE. I KNOW THAT YOU WILL. IT IS SO IMPORTANT THAT THEY REALLY LEARN HOW TO LOVE.

BE SURE TO GET PLENTY OF REST. RID YOURSELF OF THE NONESSENTIALS, BUT NEVER CLOSE YOURSELF TO SOMEONE ELSE'S NEED.

I LOVE YOU, I LOVE YOU.

The next morning, after the children had gone to school, I decided to do some more writing. It was my mother who came this time. I CAME TO TELL YOU THAT MAC IS DOING MORE FOR YOU. HE IS LEARNING SO FAST AND WANTS TO HELP YOU. REMEMBER NOW THAT I AM VERY HAPPY. DAD IS WITH ME, HE WILL COME TO YOU SOME TIME. IT IS IMPORTANT THAT THE CHILDREN LEARN TO SEE GOD IN EVERYONE, NOT TO JUDGE OTHER PEOPLE AND BE KIND AND

THOUGHTFUL TO EVERYONE. THEY WILL KNOW
GREAT JOY FROM THIS.

I had asked to be used as an instrument of good when
I began my writing. Now it was up to me to put my words
into practice. The meaning of life and death which was
given to me was meant to be shared with others. It was not
for me alone. I felt a strong obligation to give to others
what had been given to me. I wanted people to know that
when we are faced with adversity, we are given the Grace
to get through it. Grace was an old Church word which
contemporary society questioned. Call it what you will,
the meaning is still the same. God does give us an
over-powering storehouse of strength, if we choose to use
it. We need only to ask God for help—to turn to Him
instead of trying to solve everything in our small, inept,
human way. It requires humility and humbleness to admit
that we, our physical beings, are really nothing. Through
the challenges which were placed before me and the way in
which I was able to make my way through them, I knew
that I had been given tremendous help. Because of the
suffering and anguish I went through with Mac, this deep,
religious experience and understanding came. The suffering
I endured became for me an ultimate good.

As my mother said one night in her writing—THE
KNOWLEDGE THAT HAS BEEN GIVEN TO YOU IS A
GIFT THAT YOU EARNED THROUGH YOUR
SUFFERING. YOU CANNOT LOOK BACK AND FEEL
BAD BECAUSE YOUR SUFFERING TAUGHT YOU
THE THINGS THAT YOU NOW KNOW. KEEP

REMEMBERING, THE SUFFERING BROUGHT YOU THE JOY THAT YOU HAVE NOW. IT HAS BECOME THE *GOOD* IN YOUR LIFE. IT IS A CONCEPT THAT IS DIFFICULT TO TEACH PEOPLE.

You are so right Mother, I thought. It was easy for me to look back on what had happened, but it was so hard to understand while I was going through it.

I knew that it was time for me to go out and share my experience with others. But how? I wondered. Mac had written, TELL PEOPLE WHAT IT IS LIKE HERE. DESTROY THE FEAR OF DEATH AND LET THEM KNOW THE MEANING OF LIFE.

A neighbor called and asked me if I would be interested in attending a prayer meeting. I had never been to one. I was tired and had many things to do, but I felt I should go. It would be an opportunity for me to share my experience with others. I had to start somewhere.

By the time we arrived, 25 people had gathered in the small living room of a private home. They were middle-aged and younger, mostly women but a few men, from all parts of town. We sang a few songs, had some Bible readings, and then exchanged experiences. Many of the people there had received the gift of speaking in tongues. I had done some reading on this unusual gift but had never witnessed it. This phenomenon is given to a person through his devoted prayer, his meditation, and his desire to receive the Holy Spirit within himself. It involves the dedication of oneself to God. The person must ask for this gift, which often takes a long period of concentrated prayer to achieve. The gift of tongues usually occurs in spiritual surroundings and often comes as a response to a situation, as if God is answering him. The person begins speaking or chanting or singing in a strange language, the language being completely unfamiliar to him or to his past experience. Often the tone or vocal quality is different from his own natural voice. Sometimes another member of the group is given the gift of interpretation, and he knows instantly what the person is saying, even though he, too, has never heard the language before. It is a very unusual phenomenon, but it is recorded as far back as Biblical history. In the last twenty years the popularity of its significance has spread. Groups such as this have sprung up all over the country—in fact, all over the world.

One by one, those present discussed some of the experiences they had had during the week. I was extremely impressed by their selflessness, by their desire to help others in times of trouble. They were very committed to others. I could not hold myself back. I began to talk and tell my story to a room of complete strangers. My voice shook, with emotion. I realized that I would not be completely understood, but I had to take that risk. Even if only one person in the group benefited by what I said, it would be worth it. The room full of people was silent. When I had finished, a beautiful melodic chant, in a strange, foreign sounding language came from the mouth of a woman across the room. It was a fascinating, joyous, happy sound. I felt that God was rejoicing with me. Chills were running through my body. I was shivering with the grandeur of such beauty. When she had finished I felt exhausted, drained. They thanked me for sharing my experience with them. I left and went home. It had been a good night.

I continued going to the meetings for about a month, until I realized that it was quite foolish to go across town at night. I needed my rest and the children needed me home. Besides, what was really important was that groups like this spread. My own neighborhood would be a good place to start. Whether people wish to receive the gift of tongues was insignificant to me, but it was important that they understand the power of prayer, and that it take prominance in their lives.

I called a few of my neighborhood friends. Everyone was busy with the responsibilities of raising large families. Their schedules were full. No one had extra time. There were children at home and children at school. Meetings and homework were at night. Days were busy. But we would work it in. Everyone was very eager to start.

"Why is group prayer so important?" I had been asked. Mac had written: YOUR GROUP PRAYERS ARE VERY GOOD. PRAYING IN A GROUP FOR THE SAME INTENTION IS VERY POWERFUL. KEEP IT UP! Thinking about this, I looked outside. The Minnesota January had set in. Snow was piled up two-feet deep. As a car drove by, it skidded and slipped its front wheels into a snowdrift. The driver got out and looked hopelessly at the wheels buried in the snow. He got behind the car and tried pushing it with his body. The car didn't budge. Another car approached. Two teenage boys got out and offered

their help. They added their weight behind the car and
slowly it began to rock back and forth. But not enough.
The snow still held it firm. Another car came by. A man
and woman got out. She had a shovel, and the boys began
to shovel the snow from in front of the tires. The man had
some chains and he laid them down behind the wheels.
There were five people now, the driver got behind the
wheel and the four others pushed. The car began to move.
Slowly it began to gain traction and move its way back
into the clear road. It was achieved through the effort of
many.

So it was with prayer. The more people you have
praying for the same intention, the more powerful the
prayer is.

Five of us gathered together at my home one
morning. I had very few preconceived ideas of what should
happen. I knew it had to be simple, just coffee or tea,
casual clothes. I felt it was more convenient to be held at
the same time and the same house every week, so that
people would not forget. Other than that, I believed the
pattern should develop from within the group. People are
different and it was important that they be at ease and
relaxed. Some people like to sing, some like to chant, some
like to dance, and some like to read from the Bible or
other readings. Fine. "Do your own thing, ladies." I said.
So we talked. We exchanged our experiences and feelings
and opened ourselves to one another. We shared our
intentions for those we loved, around us and in the world.
We exchanged books which left us with important
messages and read passages that we enjoyed and wanted

the others to share. When we were ready, we closed our
eyes and spent five silent minutes in intense concentration
on the intentions spoken before us. We asked God to bless
our group and thanked Him for what He had given us. It
was good. It was happy. We laughed and joked. Each of us
felt richer by the experience.

Did it work?

How does one measure? Perhaps by the contentment
and peace of mind that slowly enveloped each person. It
comes with the knowledge that you are not alone. There
are those who care. There is a God who cares. You think
back to the tension and anxieties that were once with you.
Why? Why did I worry so about this? About that? It was
so small. So insignificant. So unworthy of the
apprehension that I put into it. You know your
limitations, yet the strength that comes to you helps you
to handle more than you ever could before. Fear? What is
it? Are you really afraid? If you really believe in God, fear
is no longer with you. You do the best that you can, in His
name, and that's all He asks. Nothing can scare you then.
Life becomes timeless and death a never-ending. When fear
is gone you have achieved a great oneness with God and a
potential that knows no limits.

Each of us was beginning to feel this. It reached
us at different stages, but each was feeling it in her
own way.

We felt joy as we saw those around us learning to
conquer the problems in their own lives and then turning
to help others. It is difficult to be selfless when your own
personality has conflicts within it. It is necessary to solve

your own problems first, before you will be able to give of yourself to others.

I knew that our idea of prayer had succeeded when the children would come to me and ask me to pray with them. Michael said one day, "Tommy sure was ornery today. He hit everyone. He must not be very happy. Please God help him to be happy." Sometimes they would ask the rest of the family to pray for a friend who was sick.

If the prayers in our prayer group were casual, family prayers were even more so. They lasted through most of the dinner hour and were fitted in between "Please pass the catsup" and "How come I didn't get anymore jello?" I wanted the children to understand that to pray was to speak to God. It was not important if the words weren't poetic, the rhythm smooth, or the beat melodic. The words had beauty only if they came from the heart, only if they were voluntary and spontaneous—through the mouths and in the language of children to a God who was within them and surrounded their presence. There was no set time for prayer, except at dinner. If someone had a special need, we would sit on the living room floor and all ask for help for that person. Maybe it would be in the morning when someone woke up sick. Prayer was geared to our life and our needs, and it became a part of our daily living. It was expression. In our own simple way, it was us.

We learned, too, that to vocalize our needs helped us to understand them better, and with His help they would work out. I became so bold and confident in my belief that I began to adopt the ancient practice of affirming and thanking God for His help, even before it was given.

Does it work? If you can't feel it or your intuition doesn't help you find it, perhaps you can utilize some tools of science to measure it.

Through a study group on psychic phenomena, I found that the effects of prayer could be measured scientifically. We had been discussing prayer one evening when the leader of our group, a doctor, told us about various studies that had been done on plants and the relationship of prayer to their rate of growth. Many research projects had been undertaken in this area and the results were very conclusive. Prayer did aid the growth of plants. Further studies were done under critical scientific controls, utilizing the same sensitive polygraph equipment that is also used to record human emotions (in lie detection). Electrodes from this machine were attached to the plant leaf. When the plant was threatened, the electrode marker on the machine indicated that the plant responded with a strong reaction. Tests upon tests were done on these plants and the results showed that these plants did have feelings. They responded well when they were loved. They also reacted to the sensitivities and stresses of their owners, even when the owner was miles away. It was difficult to understand that plants could have a genuine emotional relationship with people, but science was proving it.

The children and I decided to try our own experiment. We took two containers of the same size, filled them with the same amount and kind of dirt, and planted each of them with three seeds of corn. Corn was selected because it grows fast. We gave them the same amount of water, the same light and sun exposure. The only difference was that we took one container with us and kept it in our midst while we ate and prayed and were happy. We also talked to it, told it that it would grow big and strong and be beautiful. The other we would scold—tell it that it was ugly and that we didn't want it to grow. Silly it seemed. A "corny" project we agreed. We felt foolish and we laughed at ourselves for talking to plants, but we had a point to prove and we wanted to prove it. After the first week, the plant we had prayed for had three sprouts. One was an inch tall, the others three fourths of an inch high. The unloved container had only one tiny sprout, less than one fourth of an inch high. "You've gotta pray for that plant, Mom," Jimmy said. "Don'tcha know you gotta pray for that plant?" It was hard for Jimmy not to pray for everything. The growth continued in the plant we prayed for and gave love to. It was more than double the size of the other.

It was a good experiment for us to see. Not only did prayer work, but if plants were sensitive enough to respond to our love, then think how much more people must react to the attitudes of others!

My fervor for sharing my beliefs did not lessen. Things were moving too slowly for me. I wanted to reach more people. I was getting discouraged. DON'T WORRY. Mother wrote, THE LIVES OF MANY PEOPLE AROUND YOU HAVE BEEN

AFFECTED. THEY IN TURN ARE REACHING OUT TO OTHERS. IT IS GROWING!

Yes, I could see that. I saw friends and neighbors of mine sharing with others what they had learned. Through this I had met many new people in a short time. My world had grown enormously in the last few months.

It was like a flat pebble tossed into the smooth water of a lake. As the stone skips two or three times, little circles of waves begin to ripple around it. They are small at the start, but they grow and spread and eventually the gentle wavelet reaches the opposite shore. My wave was just beginning. My circle had just formed. How large would it get? Would it reach the opposite shore, or would it be like a large golden circle that would know no end?

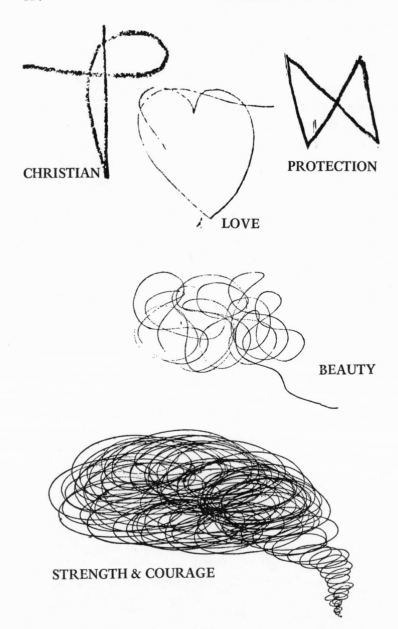

CHRISTIAN

LOVE

PROTECTION

BEAUTY

STRENGTH & COURAGE

A Cross, A Heart,
Two Triangles?

Mac's message had been: YOU SHOULD HELP OTHERS
TO UNDERSTAND WHAT IT IS LIKE HERE.

I knew that and felt it deeply. This was one of the
obligations that I had been given because of the gift of
communication I had received. Now it was up to me to
fulfill this duty.

Wherever I went, I talked and talked. As Mac had
tried to awaken people to their responsibilities to their
fellow men, I was now trying to make people aware of the
immense potential they had within themselves through
their belief in God. It was a real challenge. I talked to
friends, neighbors, relatives, and groups of people about
my experience and was eager to tell everyone my story in
the hope that it would open up new areas of meaning for
them.

Laughingly, I called myself the "white witch" of the neighborhood. Realistically, my experiences were difficult for others to understand. To people who had never heard about psychic phenomena or who had never had a psychic experience, I was obviously a very strange creature. I could sense some of their reactions when they heard about me: she's mentally ill or she has a powerful imagination. This did not really bother me, since I felt very secure and content within myself. Other people's levels of understanding had not reached the point where they could accept my experience. A few years earlier my reaction would have been much the same. My major hope now was to be able to reach some people so they could begin to read and to search for their own meanings, as I had.

I was learning to live more comfortably with the miracles that were happening to me. It seemed so natural! The automatic writing came to me easily—much more so than any other writing I do. Making out the weekly grocery list was a more difficult task than the outflow of great wisdom from my automatic writing. The grocery list required concentration and memory; what is in the refrigerator, the freezer, what shall we eat this week? Do we need any laundry soap or Kleenex? Automatic writing was exactly the opposite. It didn't require any thought process on my part. Instead it was a letting go of my own will, a blanking out of my own mind, enabling the spirit to work through me. I was nothing more than 105 pounds of pencil! My reactions at reading what I had written varied from, "Of course! Why not?" to "Good heavens! Did this really come from my hands?"

I looked at my hands. My finger nails were bitten off to an unattractive stubble. I've had the nail chewing habit for years. After trying hard to break the habit, I finally conceded that it was better than smoking. The skin was soft and translucent. Blue veins showed through and light brown spots of age were beginning to appear, reminding me that my body was growing older. My hands were small: they showed wrinkles from wringing out hundreds of diapers and from washing many windows. I was a working ant, not a queen bee.

Emotionally I felt stable. I was not lonely, depressed, or nervous, as I had been when I was absorbing the overflow of Mac's anxieties. Though I became discouraged and tired by many new responsibilities, I was glad that I was busy. If I wanted to laugh, all I had to do was look in the mirror, "Judy, you really are a kook!"

I had always been conventional. But no longer! In the short period of a few months many strange things had happened to me. My whole life had flip-flopped. With the change I became enveloped in a kind of serenity, inspired by a continuing stream of knowledge and stimulated by a torrent of courage. I awoke every morning with a sense of anticipation: "Good morning, beautiful world! What's going to happen today?"

Friends were concerned that my writing had become a crutch for me, and that I would develop into an emotional cripple who depended on the afterlife for my decisions. There were those who told me that the spirits would possess and control me. I disagreed. I had always been very independent. My will was my own. My mind was mine, to be used at my discretion. I alone was responsible to the conscience within me. I would have to take the consequences for my judgements, good and bad.

Automatic writing did not make decisions for me, but it did give me knowledge. A fantastically exciting storehouse of experience and information was alive in my fingers. It was for me to use this knowledge and use it well.

One night I attended a prayer meeting. After reading from the Bible and exchanging various experiences, the minister prayed that we be given the truth that evening. I could not contain myself—I told of my experiences. The minister asked me if it was the spirit of Christ who was working through me. I told him, "No. It was my husband."

"There is only one good spirit," he said, "the Holy Spirit. All the rest are evil. They are the works of the devil. They work in cunning ways. They appear good, but they will possess you in evil." It was useless to talk to him, he would not listen. Instead he referred to passages from the Bible concerning the Devil. The group prayed fervently for me. Surely there was a devil in their midst! I got on my broomstick and flew home!

I was confused. I knew the spirits guiding me were not bad. They had loved me on earth and continued to love me in the life beyond. Surely they would not harm me. I picked up my pen and began to write. It was Mac.

I LOVE YOU TWEETIE. I WILL WATCH OVER YOU. YOU UNDERSTAND EVERYTHING. YOU ARE RIGHT IN WHAT YOU BELIEVE. GOD IS WITH

YOU. HE IS WITH EVERYONE. WHEN YOU USE HIM AS A GUIDE YOU'LL PROGRESS EASILY AND WILL HAVE MUCH JOY AND HAPPINESS. WHEN YOU TURN AWAY FROM HIM YOU WILL HAVE TORMENTS. GOD LOVES YOU AND WANTS YOU TO BE HAPPY. THERE IS NO HELL HERE. ONLY HELL ON EARTH. HERE THERE ARE VARIOUS LEVELS OF HAPPINESS. WE HAVE TO RETURN TO THE EARTH SO WE CAN PROGRESS TO OTHER LEVELS. IT IS ONLY THRU EARTH THAT WE CAN PROGRESS. THERE IS NO DEVIL. ONLY TURNING AWAY FROM GOD.

THE CHURCH ADOPTED THE DEVIL AS A MEANS OF FORCING PEOPLE TO DO GOOD. THIS CAME ABOUT AS A MISINTERPRETATION OF THE WORDS OF CHRIST. IT WAS MEANT FOR GOOD AND HAS HELPED MANY. NOW THAT OUR LEVELS OF KNOWLEDGE HAVE INCREASED, WE ARE READY FOR A MORE COMPLETE STORY. YOU SEE, THIS COMES TO ALL OF US IN STAGES. AS YOU LOOK THRU HISTORY YOU WILL SEE WRITTEN CONCEPTS OF WHAT YOU KNOW IS TRUE. SOMEONE THEN HAD THE LIGHT TOO! YOU ARE GETTING YOURS NOW. MANY ARE NOT READY YET. SOME JUST BELIEVE BY FAITH. THIS IS A VERY PURE GIFT. IT IS INDEED GIVEN TO THE HUMBLE, THE SIMPLE, AND THE PURE IN HEART. MAN'S INCREASING INTELLIGENCE HAS PUT MANY BARRIERS TO BLIND FAITH. WE HAVE BEEN TOLD TO THINK, TO

PROBE, TO QUESTION, TO ASK WHY? EDUCATION
CAN BE A BARRIER TO FAITH BUT ALSO A VERY
USEFUL TOOL IN INFLUENCING OTHERS AND
KNOWING HOW TO USE YOUR FAITH TO HELP
OTHERS. WHAT POTENTIAL WE HAVE INSIDE OF
US, SO FEW REALIZE.

PLEASE, JUDY, DON'T BE AFRAID. WHAT I
TELL YOU IS GOOD AND BEAUTIFUL. YOU KNOW
I WOULDN'T SCARE YOU. YOU WILL BE ABLE TO
COPE WITH WHAT YOU HAVE BEEN GIVEN. YOU
WILL BE ABLE TO DO IT. YOU HAVE BEEN
TRAINED FOR THIS. IT IS LIKE A GREAT
SURGEON PERFORMING HIS MIRACLES. THEY
HAVE BEEN TRAINED TOO! YOU ARE READY FOR
THIS.

"What about the bad spirits, Mac?" I asked. YES,
THERE ARE BAD SPIRITS. I WILL PROTECT YOU
FROM THEM AND SO WILL YOUR MOTHER. WE
BOTH LOVE YOU AND WILL LET NO HARM COME
TO YOU. WE LOVE YOU. GOD LOVES YOU. YOU'RE
FOLLOWING THE RIGHT PATH. YOU CAN'T CHANGE
EVERYONE AND ARE LEARNING NOT TO TRY.
KEEP YOURSELF OPEN TO OTHER PEOPLE'S
PROBLEMS AND TRY TO REACH THEM ON THEIR
OWN LEVEL OF UNDERSTANDING. I LOVE YOU. I
LOVE YOU. I WILL PROTECT YOU.

My mind was at ease when I went to sleep that night.

During the day, my thoughts darted back to what the
minister had said about a spirit possessing me. Perhaps I

shouldn't be doing this writing, I thought. Information and comfort was what I wanted from my guides. But, I certainly desired to control my own destiny.

That night I said a short prayer, as I always did before and after doing automatic writing. Usually I said the Lord's Prayer. It was a profession of my belief. But, sometimes I just let my mind wander and said what thoughts happened to drift in. Always I asked for guidance and help from God. Mother came through this time.

DON'T WORRY ABOUT WHAT YOU ARE DOING. WE'LL NOT CONTROL YOU BUT HELP YOU TO ENRICH YOUR LIFE. WE WILL NOT LET EVIL SPIRITS COME TO YOU. IT IS TRUE THAT THEY CAN COME TO SOME PEOPLE, BUT YOU HAVE OPENED YOURSELF ONLY TO US AND WE WILL PROTECT YOU. MAC AND I WILL GUIDE YOU WITH WHAT WE HAVE LEARNED. YOU ARE AN INSTRUMENT OF GOOD, NOT BAD. WE WILL LET NO HARM COME TO YOU. GOD IS IN YOU. HE ASKS ONLY TO BE RECEIVED BY YOU. WHEN YOU RECEIVE HIM, GREAT DOORS ARE OPENED TO YOU. YOU WILL FIND EVERY DAY THAT THERE WILL BE WAYS FOR YOU TO AFFECT PEOPLE'S LIVES IN A GOD-LIKE WAY AND TO HELP THEM UNDERSTAND THEIR REASON FOR BEING. YOU WILL ALSO REALIZE, AS YOU DID LAST NIGHT, THAT OTHERS CAN'T BE REACHED ON THIS LEVEL OF UNDERSTANDING BUT HAVE TO TRAVEL A DIFFERENT ROUTE. TO UNDERSTAND COMPLETELY THAT GOD IS WITHIN EACH OF US IS

A VERY GREAT THING AND MAKES OUR
KNOWLEDGE SO MUCH MORE COMPLETE AND OUR
ROAD SO MUCH EASIER. THE BIBLE IS A GOOD
BOOK BUT THE MEANINGS HAVE BEEN
MISINTERPRETED—THE LANGUAGE HAS
CHANGED. IT CAN EASILY CONFUSE
PEOPLE. THERE ARE MANY GOOD THINGS TO BE
READ. THE BIBLE IS BY NO MEANS THE ONLY
GIFT OF GOD. GOD HAS DONE MANY, MANY
WONDERS. YOU SEE THEM AROUND YOU. YOU
ARE LIVING IN AN AURA OF GREAT LIGHT. YOU
FEEL AND KNOW GOD'S PRESENCE. HE WILL NOT
TURN YOU DOWN. WHEN YOU FOLLOW THIS
PATH, YOUR POSSIBILITIES ARE UNLIMITED. YOU
HAVE A LOT OF WORK AHEAD OF YOU. IT WILL
BE BEAUTIFUL—RICH AND MEANINGFUL. YOU
WERE NEVER INTERESTED IN JUST
EXISTING. YOU HAVE ALWAYS BEEN A PERSON
WHO WANTED TO HELP. NOW YOU WILL FIND
WAYS TO HELP MORE. YOU WILL BE HAPPY
BECAUSE OF THIS. FRUSTRATIONS COME WHEN
YOU CAN'T HELP. THEN YOU MUST REALIZE
THAT THIS IS MEANT TO TEACH YOU. THRU THIS
YOU WILL LEARN AND PROGRESS. LIFE IS
LEARNING—LEARNING SO WE CAN HAVE THE
WISDOM OF GOD AND BE ABLE TO RETURN TO
HIM. DON'T CONCERN YOURSELF WITH
NEGATIVISM AND NEGATIVE SPIRITS. THIS IS
OPERATING IN A NEGATIVE WAY. GOD IS
GOOD. HE WANTS EVERYTHING GOOD FOR

US. THE DEVIL DOES NOT <u>EXIST!</u> THIS IS ONLY WHEN PEOPLE TURN AWAY FROM GOD. THEN THEY HAVE LESSONS TO LEARN. PEOPLE WILL TRY TO TALK YOU INTO THIS DEVIL CONCEPT BUT KEEP REMEMBERING—<u>GOD IS GOOD!</u> THIS IS ALL FOR NOW. YOU ARE DOING SO WELL. I WEEP FOR JOY. I LOVE YOU DEAR.

God is good! The Devil does not exist! God is Good! The words were large and emphatic on the paper. They were underlined many times in dark, heavy lines. My hands felt the emotional intensity that was coming through to me from my Mother. My spirits could not speak and show their extreme feelings by the raising of their voices, but there was no question in my mind that my hand was recording a very deep and affirmative statement.

Even while my spirit guides told me not to worry, I could not forget about negative influences. I was hearing more and more about the experiences other people had with bad spirits.

The secret world of psychic individuals was opening up to me. People who have had experiences like mine were very reluctant to discuss them with those who hadn't; they could be misunderstood so easily. No one wanted to be judged as queer. But it was exciting for me to be able to discuss my experiences with such individuals. Communication is vital to us all.

I enrolled in a seminar on psychic phenomena at the University of Minnesota and another series of courses on the occult at a study center. It was very comforting to me to see that when I was with psychic individuals, my automatic writing was accepted as very ordinary. With them I was not a freak! Psychic people were no different from anyone else. I met hypnotists, trance mediums, psychic readers, palmists, astrologers, gurus, and healers. There wery men and women, from teenagers to old people who were short and fat, tall and thin, crippled and strong, rich and poor. They were people. Their psychic gifts had not led them to perfection, but they had been given understanding and a rich sense of awareness to their roles in life. In most of these people their purpose was a dedication to others and a love of God. They were beautiful in spirit and in word. I loved them!

As I heard their stories, I learned more about negative spirits. When one is open to spirit communication, anything can enter. It's like opening the door to your home and advertising "Welcome world, come on in." How many really bad people have you known in life? I didn't think that I knew any, but the newspapers were full of murders and stories of misguided people of criminal intent. I certainly didn't want them in my house. The personalities that we have in life we carry through after death into the life of the world beyond. The threshold of death enlightens and educates everyone, but some spirits are so attached to this world in a materialistic way that they do not turn toward the light for greater spiritual enrichment and learning. These spirits are in the dark. The only company they have is that of other selfish souls. Given an opportunity to work through an earth being excites them. As there are selfish, cruel people on earth, so are there the "evil spirits." People who work with spirits have to be very careful to prevent bad spirits from entering. They can be cunning, mischievous, and very clever. They are the crooks, the gangsters, the dope pushers, and the criminals of our earth level. They are the opportunists, who have used other people for their own gain. When they die, they may not wish to grow spiritually but may prefer to stay closely attached to the earth level and continue with their ways. It is very important for people who engage in spirit communication to protect themselves through prayer, in order to keep their own spiritual level high. Spirits can be your friends or enemies.

The ouija board, a very old tool of communication, has been increasing in popularity. It can become an excellent mechanism through which a spirit might develop control over a person. The board has the letters of the alphabet on it. Two people place their hands on either side of a pointer, and the spirit allegedly spells out a word by guiding the pointer through their hands. I have used it and have achieved good results with it. It was amazing how fast the pointer would move to spell out words and develop messages. However, I had been given warning not to use it again, since it was difficult to identify the spirits and to know their intention. It also is easy for an entity to pick up your own thoughts through mental telepathy and transfer them onto the board. For example, I heard about the experience of a girl who picked up a spirit through a ouija board. She had become very receptive to the influences of the spirit whom she called Dave. Dave began to give her much counsel and advice. Unfortunately, none of it was good. She had been leading a promiscuous life when she encountered him. He encouraged her further with her liasons with married men. "You won't get caught," he assured her. "Don't worry, you won't get caught." These alliances that she had with men, encouraged by Dave, caused her much mental anguish and confusion. He was not much help to her. Dave's presence soon became obvious to others who knew her. Friends of hers had witnessed the activities of poltergeists—the phenomenan of objects being moved by an unseen force. Many people had seen coffee cups and ashtrays travel across her bedroom by themselves.

A friend called one day to tell me of the strange experiences he has had since moving to a new home. The carpenter who was doing some remodeling had said, "If I didn't know better, I'd think this house was haunted. I sure hear a lot of unusual noises." The family had a teenage boy, Dick, who admitted that he had been seeing a spirit—it was of a boy, who appeared to be a little older than he. "There was another spirit too," he said. "An older person." As Dick described the second spirit, his father realized it was the boy's grandfather, whom Dick had never seen when he was alive. Apparently the younger spirit was telling the boy to do things which the grandfather did not approve of. A fight was on. The young spirit told him to do one thing, the grandfather told him something else. Dick's father called the previous owners of the house and asked them if they had a son. They said that they had, but their son had been in trouble and the family had not seen him for a long time. The description of their son fit perfectly the spirit Dick had described. The family said that their boy had been a professional drummer and that the last car he owned had been blue. The spirit had told Dick that he had been killed in a blue car and that he would help him to learn to play the drums. Two years earlier Dick had taken music lessons but had given up, as his teacher had told him that he didn't have any natural ability. But now he was astounding everyone with his amazing talent at the drums! Evidently the spirit had come back to its old home, only to find it inhabited by another young boy, whom he soon found he could have some fun with. The parents of the spirit had not known of the boy's death. They had tried to trace him but had been unsuccessful. Dick's father was uncomfortable as he explained the situation to the spirit's family. It was a very shocking and unusual way for the father of the spirit to discover that his missing son had departed from this world and that he was now haunting his old home.

This spirit had been causing a lot of unusual commotion around the house. Late at night the family would hear the electric garage doors open and the sound of a car driving into the garage. The car would come to a stop and the motor would be turned off. Then the garage door would close. What made it strange was that the garage doors did not actually open nor did a car drive in. The sounds were unmistakable though. Everyone in the family heard them.

Although the sounds of the garage doors opening and closing at night continued, other things were going on too.

While Dick's mother was home alone during the day, the water faucets would turn on, toilets would flush, and door bells would ring.

Often the family would hear footsteps in the hall. They would hurry to look but no one was there. The house was small. They could surely have seen someone if there was someone to see. Perhaps the most perplexing manifestation was the heavy footsteps that the family heard going back and forth along the ceilings of the bedrooms. Above the bedrooms was an attic, which was too low for anyone to stand up in. Off and on the footsteps would be heard, to the bewilderment of the occupants below.

One night the furniture in the amusement room began moving, banging into other furniture. The heavy pool table would slide back and forth across the floor. This was not as annoying to the family as the noises of large trucks which they heard many nights. It sounded as though large vans and trucks were racing through their living room. Neither the stereo set turned on high nor the television set at its loudest volume could drown out the truck sounds. The noise was not conductive to a good night's sleep.

As the spirit began to bother Dick more and more he became quite disturbed. The family made the decision to sell the house and move out. After they had listed the house with a real estate agent and put an ad in the paper, things began to quiet down. But before they could move, they felt a different presence. The smell of breakfast awakened them each morning—fresh toast, bacon frying, and eggs cooking. Once Dick's mother noticed the aroma of what smelled to her like oatmeal cookies baking. How nice to have a spirit which liked to bake! At least it was better than one who drives trucks. It was all so strange, but stranger still when one lived in that house and smelled the aromas and listened to the noises.

The haunting of houses does not necessarily mean that there are bad entities involved. Sometimes a spirit is attached materialistically to a house that it did not want to leave. Perhaps its experiences there were happy and it wanted to stay and relive in another way its past existence. Occasionally there are spirits which become attached to the people living in the home. Small children make good receivers for communication from spirits, because children have not built up a wall of skepticism, as most adults have. Sometimes the "imaginary friends" children have are not so imaginary at all but are real spirits which are able to manifest themselves only through the eyes of a child.

I have never seen a spirit. Many, many people have. Hans Holzer, a leading researcher and writer about the occult, has recently written a book on psychic photography. Captured on a photograph, spirit manifestations appear quite convincing. A physical manifestation requires the ability to see the subject. The mechanics involved, as explained to me, are similar to the electronics of a television set. The picture is recorded by the studio (spirit) and then broken down into infintesimal pieces which are carried across the air waves. These fragments are picked up by the receiver and put together in the receiver's mind to form a picture. This explains why not everyone is able to see an apparition. A spirit may manifest itself physically and be seen by some and not seen by others. The people who see this phenomenon have developed within themselves this ability to put the picture together, quite to their own shock and surprise. Some students of metaphysics clalim that this unusual ability develops because of differences in the chemical components of our bodies.

In Hans Holzer's book, there are pictures in which ectoplasm is seen leaving the body of a trance medium to form the physical manifestation of a spirit or "ghost" as we sometimes call them. This ectoplasm is the "raw material" out of which a materialization of the dead is created. It is a white albumen-like substance that has been analyzed in laboratories and is drawn from a medium during seances.

Apparitions can come for many reasons, good or bad, The apparitions that stay on earth as ghosts are wasting their time. They are depriving their souls of the spiritual growth and learning that they need to rise to the ultimate level of fullness with God.

We can help these souls find their way to enlightenment through our prayers. There is good reason why the church has commended us to pray for the dead. The souls which have gone beyond need help too! In my automatic writing, I asked Mac what I could do for him. PRAY FOR ME, he wrote. We all need help, the living and the dead, through prayer.

It became obvious to me, through the experience of others, that automatic writing could be a source of mischievousness and harm. A woman whom I'd met in a class called to say that she had begun to do automatic writing and was getting results. Relatives had come through to her and had identified themselves in distinct ways. Her grandmother wrote in a manner of speech similar to that which she had used in life. The woman was quite certain that it was her grandmother. The messenger had described events and situations that had taken place which could easily be checked out. However, next came a message purporting to be from her mother—YOU WILL BE WITH US AT CHRISTMAS TIME! The woman's thought that she was going to die at Christmas was hardly a pleasant one. She called me for help. It did not sound right to me. While she waited on the phone, I did some automatic writing. Mac signed in, TWEETIE, NO ONE WHO LOVES YOU WOULD WANT TO SCARE YOU. IT SOUNDS LIKE SOMEONE IS PLAYING WITH HER. TELL HER THAT SHE SHOULD LEAVE IT ALONE.

Spirits use the same pet names and cliches that they did in life. This is helpful in knowing with whom you are communicating. Mac writes "Tweetie", my mother "Dear", just as they did in life.

I was very amused one day. I had an argument with a relative of my mother concerning some money. There were things that I had wanted to say to her for a long time, but I'd held back in order not to hurt her feelings. The day she called I'd finally had enough! I vented the wrath which had been mounting for years. I felt my mother's presence pushing me on and on. I really let go and said everything that welled up inside me. After her phone call, I did some automatic writing. Mother came through in large explosive, pulsating letters. She wrote GREAT! GREAT! THAT'S WHAT SHE NEEDED. LET HER STEW IN HER OWN JUICE FOR AWHILE! "Let her stew in her own juice!" I laughed and laughed. I hadn't heard that expression in years. How many times I had heard my mother say it. Little did my relative know that she had two women to deal with instead of just one.

Spirits can make mistakes. In the other world, as in life, they are not perfect. They are learning and growing in wisdom, as we are. One of their greatest helps is their ability to break the time barrier. They can see what is going to happen! However, there are things that can change and alter paths that had seemed, by design, to be unchangeable. One can make a dental appointment, write it down on the calendar, and tell the family you are going to the dentist on Tuesday. Tuesday morning arrives, you wake up with a temperature. It's the flu, so you cancel the dentist appointment. Such are the ways of life. The plans that we make can be changed. In the same way, destiny can sometimes be thwarted. Premonitions that some people have had have saved lives. Yet others, such as Jeane Dixon's vision of the death of President Kennedy, have not averted tragedy already set in motion.

I waited expectantly for the wedding of a relative which my mother had written would take place on November 12. November 12 came and went, and no wedding bells were heard. He finally was married in July, which is a long time from November. It is very difficult to be accurate with time in the spirit world.

There were also occasions when confusion reigned because I misinterpreted the writing. One night I asked Mac if Kevin would go to a certain ski race. He wrote, YES, I SEE HIM THERE. We were very excited to think that Kevin would not be disqualified and that he would go on to the race. However, we were wrong. Kevin did not qualify for the race. But he did attend, and he did ski. His father was right; he did "see" him at the race but not as a contender. It was our error. Receiving a message through automatic writing requires a careful understanding of the words used. As in Mac's message about homework to Kevin, it could be interpreted in different ways.

Mistakes would be made. Whether it was through time, word misinterpretation, or my judgment or theirs, errors would occur. The greatest psychic of the twentieth century, Edgar Cayce, was given credit for 90% accuracy. I could surely be satisfied with much less. For when I receive correct information that I could not have possibly known by myself, it is an exciting experience, and I am learning to accept the disappointments of my mistakes.

There is another area where spirits can help us. Mac often wrote me what people were thinking. "How come you always know?" I asked him one day. TWEETIE, IT'S LIKE THIS—SPIRITS CAN GET INSIDE PEOPLE AND TELL WHAT'S GOING ON IN THEIR MINDS. THEY CAN TELL WHAT PEOPLE ARE THINKING. WE ARE NOT HAMPERED BY THEIR PHYSICAL BODY SO WE

CAN DEAL DIRECTLY WITH YOUR MIND LEVEL. IT
DOES NOT MATTER WHAT PEOPLE ARE
SAYING – WE KNOW WHAT THEY ARE
THINKING. "Wow!" I thought to myself. "You sure
must have fun! I'm not going to feel sorry for
you!"

Spirit communications can be helpful or harmful, or
they may amount to nothing. It depends largely on one's
motives. If a person considers it a game, it would perhaps
be better to take up tennis. If spirit communication is for
amusement only, it would be better to see a movie. if one
pursues it solely as an intellectual exercise, one might be
better off reading a good book.

Psychic abilities, like any other talent, are neutral in
direction. Because of free will the person receiving this gift
has the choice to use it in a positive or negative way; to
help himself and others, or for harm.

The world of the occult has a large attraction to all
because of the magnitude and variety of powers it can give.
When these abilities are received by misguided or confused
people the resulting consequences can be dangerous to
themselves and to society. There are people who are
developing their psychic talents and/or using mind
expanding drugs or hallucinogens to increase their level of
consciousness. Many are using this as a form of escape,
because they are unable to cope with the frustrations and
realities of their everyday lives. For some, new concepts of
evil are developed in their disoriented minds. Evil is
understood as a dynamic force in itself.

Throughout our country cults are being formed for the worship of the devil. Elaborate ceremonies are performed to ward off the spirit of this power. The rites of ancient cultures are being brought back with black witchcraft, black masses, sexual perversion, and the worship of Satan. Potions, amulets, upside down crucifixes, vampires, and symbols of death are all a part of this culture. Stories of the offering of animal and sometimes human sacrifices to the altar of Satan are in our news media today. It is frightening, shocking, and bewildering to us all. While most realize the bizarreness of it, there are others who live in real fear and under the shadow of its ominous blackness.

It is best that we all understand that the direction of one's psychic abilities lies in the hands of the individual. It will be guided to good or bad by his own free will and intellect.

In my first attempt at communication, I had asked in devout prayer to be used as an instrument of good to help others. IF YOU WANT TO USE THIS SELFISHLY, I WOULD HAVE TO STOP AS I WOULD BE HARMING BOTH YOU AND ME. YOU HAVE ASKED TO BE USED TO HELP OTHERS AND YOU SHALL. FOR BY HELPING YOU, WE HELP OUR SPIRITS TOO! Mac had written. Mother and Mac had declared that they would protect me from bad spirits. I believed them but was always on guard for something different in my writing that could mean another personality, possibly a negative one, had come through.

Communicating with my loved ones in the after life is interesting to me. However, it is not right to place too much emphasis on the life beyond. The dead can never take the place of the living in human relations. Fortunately, I have many friends to rely on for social outlet, and five children to absorb my energy.

The here and now not only fulfills me but is also very demanding—like yesterday when I received a call from the school nurse . . .

"Kevin has injured his leg playing football and I think it should be X-rayed," she said.

As we sat in the waiting room at the hospital, Kevin was worried and apprehensive.

"Mom, this is the third time this fall that I've been in this emergency room," he complained.

"Well at least today you don't have to be stitched up. For awhile I was afraid that you were going to look like a survivor of the Civil War with all of the scars on your head." I said.

"Ahh mom, they don't really show. My hair covers them up. Besides it's not only me. Mary had her chin stitched up when she fell off her bike a few weeks ago and Jimmy . . .Jimmy's been to the hospital twice for stiches lately. Didn't he have his head X-rayed too?"

"Yes, he was knocked out when he hit his head on the marble table. He came close to a concussion that time. I'm afraid his head is going to be as banged up as yours."

"Remember Michael had that terrible black eye right after dad died when . . .

The nurse interrupted. "Mrs. McCarthy, the X-rays are all right. Kevin can leave now."

With relief I filled out hospital insurance forms, a process I had repeated nine times in the last nine months.

While the children's accidents were not serious, they certainly weren't enjoyable either. Life was not easy for me and often I would get very discouraged. There was not time for relaxation and fun seemed a part of another world.

DON'T WORRY, Mac would write, YOU'RE GOING TO HAVE A GOOD LIFE. YOU'LL HAVE FUN AGAIN. YOU ARE RECEIVING MUCH HELP FROM MANY OF US.

Much help? I need it! My morale had kept up for three months without sagging, but I was still so tired. "Whoever you are," I complained, "if you're helping me, there seems to be a lousy division of labor. You couldn't be as tired out as I. Besides, who are the 'many of us' that Mac refers to?"

There were other questions I had too. Mac had mentioned the various levels of existence where he was. I wondered what he really meant by that. Jesus said, "In my Father's house there are many mansions . . ." I couldn't remember the rest. I wondered if Jesus was referring to the levels that Mac wrote about? I decided to do some writing and find out. YES, TWEETIE, WE CAN HELP YOU. Ah ha! I thought at last I'm going to find out who "we" is. I put my pencil down on the paper. I AM ONE OF YOUR OTHER GUIDES. I AM VERY IMPORTANT

FOR YOU. I WILL HELP YOU NOW WITH OTHER
QUESTIONS THAT YOU HAVE. What is your name? I
asked. MY NAME IS NOT IMPORTANT TO YOU. I
was suspicious. The guide might think it wasn't important
but to me it was. I wanted to know with whom I was
working. I let the writing continue. A strange sign began to
form on the paper. It was like a cross, yet different. THIS
IS MY SYMBOL FOR YOU. IN MY FATHER'S HOUSE
ARE MANY MANSIONS. I WILL GO AND PREPARE A
PLACE FOR YOU. THIS IS WHAT WE ALSO MEAN
BY LEVELS. THERE ARE PLACES FOR EVERYONE
ACCORDING TO THE PROGRESS OF HIS SOUL. IT IS
THE SAME AS SCHOOL WITH TEACHERS FOR
EVERY LEVEL AND PEOPLE THAT ARE ON YOUR
LEVEL TO HELP AND WORK WITH YOU. THIS IS
VERY IMPORTANT. YOU MUST NOT FORGET
THIS. AS YOU KNOW THE ULTIMATE GOAL IS THE
SPIRITUAL PERFECTION OF YOUR SOUL. THIS IS
ACHIEVED BY THE GOOD WE DO ON EARTH. THIS
IS WHY THE EARTH ROLE IS SO IMPORTANT. OUR
SOUL CANNOT PROGRESS AS WELL IN THE
HEREAFTER. THE HEREAFTER IS FOR LEARNING
TOO BUT THE REAL PROGRESS IS DONE ON
EARTH. WHEN YOU FIRST DIE YOUR SOUL IS
HELPED BY OTHER UNDERSTANDING SOULS TO
LEARN THEIR NEW ROLE. IT IS LIKE ON EARTH
WHEN YOU ENTER A NEW PHASE OF YOUR LIFE
SUCH AS THE ROLE OF MARRIAGE OR GIVING
BIRTH TO A CHILD. YOU ARE GIVEN LESSONS TO
PREPARE FOR YOUR NEW ROLE. IT IS THE SAME

HERE. NOW IT IS TRUE THERE ARE STUBBORN SPIRITS THAT REFUSE TO LISTEN AND STAY FIRMLY ATTACHED TO THE EARTH LEVEL. THESE ARE YOUR GHOSTS. THERE ARE ALSO SPIRITS THAT CHOOSE TO WORK CLOSELY WITH EARTH PEOPLE IN ORDER TO COMPLETE UNFINISHED WORK. IT IS ALSO TRUE THAT SOME SPIRITS ARE NOT HELPFUL. AS THERE ARE PEOPLE WITH BAD IDEALS SO THERE ARE SPIRITS WITH BAD IDEALS. NOW YOU ARE BEING CAREFULLY PROTECTED, SO YOU MUSTN'T WORRY ABOUT THESE. HOWEVER A WARNING MUST BE GIVEN THAT ANYONE WHO OPENS HIMSELF TO COMMUNICATIONS WITH THE SPIRIT WORLD CAN PICK UP A BAD SPIRIT. NOW THE THING TO TELL PEOPLE IS TO KNOW THAT SPIRIT COMMUNICATIONS ARE NOT FOR EVERYONE. THIS IS TRUE. IT CAN DEFINITELY BE HARMFUL TO CERTAIN INDIVIDUALS. PLEASE KNOW THAT YOU ARE BEING HELPED IN MANY WAYS. WE ARE HELPING YOU BECAUSE YOU ARE VERY IMPORTANT TO US NOW. THE SYMBOL I USE IS THE ANCIENT SYMBOL OF CHRIST. SO YOU KNOW THAT I AM A CHRISTIAN.

I WANT TO TELL YOU MORE ABOUT THE LEVELS WE HAVE HERE. A SPIRIT STAYS ON ONE LEVEL ACCORDING TO HIS SPIRITUAL GROWTH. WHEN HE IS READY HE MAY CHOOSE TO GO TO ANOTHER LEVEL. OF COURSE HE CANNOT GO UNTIL HE HAS LEARNED WHAT HE

SHOULD. NOW YOU HAVE CALLED THIS PURGATORY. THIS IS A NEGATIVE UNDERSTANDING THAT IS NOT REALLY TRUE AS WE HAVE GREAT LIGHT AND UNDERSTANDING AT THIS LEVEL. IT MUST BE MADE VERY CLEAR THAT THE HELL YOU GO THRU IS BECAUSE OF YOUR PAST MISTAKES AND THIS TAKES PLACE ON EARTH. THERE IS NO HELL HERE. IT IS NOT NEGATIVE, BUT THE GREATER HAPPINESS THAT WE ACHIEVE HERE IS MORE A ONENESS WITH GOD. THIS COMES WITH THE GROWTH THAT WE ACHIEVE IN LIFE. LIFE IS LEARNING AS IS OUR EXISTENCE. IT IS LIKE LISTENING TO A BEAUTIFUL ORCHESTRA. THE MORE ONE KNOWS AND UNDERSTANDS AND APPRECIATES MUSIC THE RICHER THE EXPERIENCE. SO KNOWLEDGE DOES PLAY A VERY IMPORTANT ROLE IN OUR LIVES. BUT KNOWLEDGE IS ACHIEVED IN MANY WAYS. THRU BOOKS AND THRU EXPERIENCE. IT IS VERY IMPORTANT TO NEVER FORGET TO ASK YOURSELF AFTER HAVING GONE THRU A DIFFICULT EXPERIENCE—"WHAT CAN I LEARN FROM THIS? HOW CAN I USE THIS EXPERIENCE TO MAKE ME A BETTER PERSON?" BECAUSE IF WE DON'T LEARN ANYTHING THRU THAT EXPERIENCE WE WILL HAVE TO BE GIVEN ANOTHER. LIFE IS LEARNING. LEARNING HOW TO PERFECT OURSELVES SO WE WILL BE ABLE TO BECOME ONE WITH GOD. He was through. The pencil ran off the paper. I thanked him. Or it. Or whatever. "O.K." I said,

"Is there anyone else?" My hand began moving in round circular motions. The pencil responded differently than it ever had before. Round swirly lines were forming a pattern. The writing began. The lines were round, fat and circular. The someone coming through was quite fancy! I AM SOMEONE NEW FOR YOU. I WANT YOU TO SEE THAT I AM A LITTLE DIFFERENT. I should say you are different, I thought. I AM THE ONE THAT WILL HELP YOU STAY BEAUTIFUL. AREN'T I PRETTY? Oh, this is silly, I thought. But the writing continued. I WANT YOU TO KNOW THAT YOUR BEAUTY IS ALSO IMPORTANT BECAUSE YOU ARE THE HOLDER OF BEAUTIFUL TRUTHS. YOUR SPIRITUAL, MENTAL, AND PHYSICAL BEAUTY IS IMPORTANT. THERE IS NOTHING MORE NOW. Say, wait a minute, I giggled. Beauty counselor, what am I going to do about the dry skin? I laughed—this was ridiculous! However, my hand was still moving rapidly. Another sign was being formed. Goodness! If I had known I was going to have a party, at least I would have dressed properly. I had another spirit. A drawing appeared. Two triangles were formed into something like the shape of a butterfly. Another shape was made. Then another. Then the writing began. I AM HERE TO PROTECT YOU. YOU ARE IMPORTANT TO US. I AM YOUR PROTECTOR. YOUR HUSBAND WORKS WITH ME TO TAKE GOOD CARE OF YOU AND I WILL BE WITH YOU THE REST OF YOUR LIFE. I AM PLEASED THAT I HAVE SUCH A JOB. Before I could figure out the triangle or even say thank you, another sign was made.

This looked something like a large "P". THIS IS A SYMBOL FOR HONESTY. I AM TO HELP YOU SO THAT YOU DON'T ERR IN THE TRUTHS. IF YOU EVER QUESTION THE VALIDITY OF SOMETHING ASK FOR HONESTY. I WILL GIVE YOU THE CORRECT ANSWER. Then another sign was coming! Large, strong, black circles were made. This was something strong. Again the writing was different from the others. I WILL GIVE YOU COURAGE AND STRENGTH. JUST ASK. That was all. Nothing more. You sure will hear from me, I thought. My hand kept moving. A large heart was made. I AM CONCERNED ABOUT YOUR LOVE. I KNOW THAT WILL MAKE YOU HAPPY. WE WANT FOR YOU TO BE HAPPY AND YOU WILL. Hey, wait a minute. Now, here was someone I really wanted some information from. But there was no more. The writing had stopped. The party was over.

I looked at the clock. Hardly 15 minutes had passed since I had first started writing. I was tired. The writing had exhausted me. I said a short prayer of thanks and fell asleep.

HONESTY

Shine With Faith

"Marilyn, how do I tell people that I'm corresponding with a cross, a heart and two triangles?" I asked my good friend the next day over a cup of coffee.

"Well," she laughed, "If you're smart, you won't tell anyone—they'd think you're crazy."

"O.K.—so I'm not so smart," I said. "Now what'll I do? I have to let people know about what has happened to me. Even if they don't believe me, they still might be able to get some idea of the potential they have within themselves."

"Maybe you could write about what has happened. Say, why don't you write a book? Get that automatic hand to work!"

"Me? Me, write a book? Impossible! I couldn't write a book."

"Why? Why not?" she challenged.

"I haven't written since I was in college—and that was longer ago than I care to think about."

"Remember," she argued, "you had never written automatically a few months ago either."

"But, I've got so much work now—I have at least a hundred thank you notes left from the funeral and an endless list of things to get caught up with. I wish Mac had gotten the storm windows up and the leaves raked before he left."

"Very inconsiderate of him," she chuckled.

"Time, that's all I need is a lot of time—and at least two more of me." I moaned.

"Well, time you'll get. And help too, I'll bet. Think about it," she said as she left.

I did think about it. All day long I thought of how I had committed myself to automatic writing to help others. Yet how difficult it was to tell people what I'm doing. I had had a treasure of jewels that I wanted to give away, but I couldn't . . . Or could I? Could I possibly write about what has happened to me? But how? How could I possibly do it?

That night I went to bed with troubled thoughts on my mind. In a half sleep I began to think of stacks and stacks of beautiful books floating on fluffy white clouds. Their paper was shiny new, and the colors were bright and vivid. They were all written by me! They were all done! On the cover of each one was the picture of Mac. His face was smiling and eyes were twinkling, compelling the reader to pick up the book. He seemed to be saying, "Read me, people. Read my book! Hear what I have to say. I can't talk to you anymore, nor can I sing, or cry, or joke, or dance. You can't see the tears in my eyes or hear my voice throbbing with emotion as I talk to you, but . . . but, I can write! I can write to you, my friends, the people that I love. I can write to you and tell you that I still love you, that I still care about you, and that I am still with you. I can write and tell you what I know now—so much more than I did before. I can write! So read me. Read me, my friends—read what I have to tell you."

I awoke in the middle of the night and knew then that I would write a book. The "how" didn't matter, just the "will", and at that moment I willed myself to do it. I went back to sleep, satisfied. On awakening the next morning, reality had set in. The "how" became very important. After the children had gone to school, Jimmy and I went shopping. I bought a typewriter, a large stack of paper, more pencils, and many more erasers. "Now all I need is a gigantic wastebasket," I said to myself as I cleared off my desk. The only way to write, was to write. I tore off a sheet of paper and started.

My book had begun! My secrets would come out. My feelings, my emotions, my guts were being turned inside out and presented to the outside world. Whether I liked it or not, I would be judged by everyone who read my words. My anonymity would come to an end. My cocoon days were over, and whether I emerged as a lowly moth or a brilliant butterfly, I did not care. For I was writing. My thoughts exploded through my fingers and I wrote and wrote.

There are psychiatrists who assert that the mind is used to only ten percent of its capacity. They say that the conscious mind is, for the most part, sleeping. We all are aware that we have latent talents deep inside of us. "Wake up, sleepy mind!" I commanded. "Wake up, you lazy mind, and get to work." If there were powers and talents inside of me, then it was time they were used. "All right," I said, "it's going to take everything I have to do this, so get going—get to work."

I lay in bed that night, excited and exhilarated about my new role. I took paper and pencil to find out what Mac's reaction would be to my decision. IT WILL BE GREAT, TWEETIE, he wrote. YOU HAVE RECEIVED SUCH GOOD INFORMATION THAT YOU CAN USE AND WE WILL GET YOU MORE. YOU WON'T BE DOING THIS BY YOURSELF BUT WILL RECEIVE LOTS OF HELP. WE HAVE TO CONVINCE PEOPLE THAT THIS IS TRUE. IT IS SO IMPORTANT FOR PEOPLE TO KNOW THIS. IT WILL HELP THEM TO LEAD MORE MEANINGFUL LIVES AND WILL HELP TO BUILD A BETTER WORLD. THE FEAR OF DEATH HAS TO BE ELIMINATED AND THE MEANING OF LIFE HAS TO BE KNOWN. IT IS HARD TO CONVINCE PEOPLE BUT WITH A BOOK YOU COULD. I WANT THE BOOK TO EMBODY MY IDEALS AND DREAMS TOO! I TRIED TO BE LIKE JESUS BUT I COULDN'T. I TRIED BUT I WAS TOO WEAK. NOW I CAN REALLY DO THINGS. IT IS SO EXCITING.

Kathleen and Mary were bouncing and giggling in their room next to mine. It was late, and they bothered me. I yelled for them to be quiet in a loud, strong voice. Suddenly Mac was gone. The pencil didn't write. After a few minutes the writing began again. TWEETIE WE ALMOST LOST OUR COMMUNICATION. I CAN'T WORK WITH YOU WHEN YOU YELL AT THE CHILDREN. YOU KNOW I NEVER LIKED THAT. "Fine," I said, "then you yell at them." That will fix him, I giggled. There's really not much you can do about it anyway. At last I have the final word! "I'm sorry," I laughed. "I guess we can still argue. Now what were you saying?" I FELT SO BAD WHEN I REALIZED THAT I HAD LEFT YOU. IT WAS SO UNFAIR FOR YOU TO HAVE TO RAISE THE CHILDREN ALONE, BUT WHEN I FOUND OUT I COULD WORK WITH YOU AGAIN I WAS HAPPY. I WAS NEVER HAPPY ON EARTH LIKE I AM HERE. IT IS SO BEAUTIFUL TO BE ABLE TO WORK LIKE I CAN WITHOUT ALL OF THOSE EARTHLY FRUSTRATIONS. AND I THOUGHT SKIING WAS GREAT! WHAT A LAUGH! He did not sign off in his usual, I LOVE YOU. There seemed to be something different coming. The pencil began to move in circles again. The big, beautiful spiraling circles that I had received when I had first begun to write appeared on the paper. They were called circles of joy, and I agreed. I felt joy within me. I had someone new writing. Who was it? It was someone good, I knew, because of the happiness that I felt radiating throughout my body. The circles kept coming,

but they were changing to form letters. I'M YOUR
FATHER. I looked at the words, and the tears rolled
down my face. He had been dead for twenty years. I
remembered him only as a sweet, faint memory. The
writing continued, I was throbbing with emotion. YES, IT
IS ME. I HAVE BEEN WATCHING YOU
CLOSELY. YOU HAD A PRETTY BAD TIME FOR
AWHILE. YOU DID VERY WELL THOUGH. YOU
PASSED YOUR TESTS, THAT IS WHY YOU HAVE
BEEN GIVEN THIS. NOW I WILL BE ABLE TO HELP
YOU WITH YOUR BOOK. YOU ARE VERY MUCH
LIKE ME AND I'LL BE ABLE TO GIVE YOU SOME
GOOD IDEAS. IT'S BEEN A GOOD LONG TIME
SINCE WE'VE TALKED. I CAN REMEMBER WHEN
YOU WERE A CHILD AND YOU WOULD SIT ON MY
LAP WHILE I WROTE AND READ. WE BOTH LIKED
TO READ AND TO WRITE. I CAN REMEMBER HOW I
USED TO TUCK YOUR HAIR BEHIND YOUR
EAR. YOU NEVER LIKED THAT. BUT YOU DID
LIKE TO SIT ON MY LAP. I'VE WATCHED OVER
YOU FOR A LONG TIME AND I'VE BEEN PROUD OF
YOU. PLEASE KNOW HOW HARD MAC IS WORKING
FOR YOU. YOU HAVE A LOT OF WORK TO DO,
MORE THAN ANY OF US HAD TO DO ON EARTH
BUT YOU WON'T BE DOING IT ALONE. YOU WERE
SELECTED FOR THIS BECAUSE YOU'VE DONE
WELL. YOU DESIRED TO BE AN INSTRUMENT OF
GOOD! THIS IS WONDERFUL. WE WERE SO HAPPY
WHEN WE HEARD OF THIS. YOUR PRAYERS HAVE
BEEN HEARD AND WILL BE ANSWERED. YOU WILL

HAVE THE POWER OF GOD AND YOU KNOW IT IS NOT YOURS, BUT HIS. HE WILL USE YOU AS HE DESIRES. YOU HAVE A BUSY LIFE AHEAD. SHED ALL OF THE UNIMPORTANT THINGS IN YOUR LIFE. WE WANTED SO BADLY TO HELP YOU AND NOW THAT WE SEE YOU'RE ON THE RIGHT ROAD AND ARE OPEN TO US, WE CAN DO IT. WHAT EXCITEMENT! EVERYONE IS OVERJOYED WITH YOU. WE WILL ALL HELP YOU! THATS ALL FOR NOW . . . YOUR FATHER.

It had been a big day. I put the pencil down, said a prayer of thanks, and fell fast asleep.

When I woke the next morning I read and reread what I had written. I felt I should write some more. Again I took the paper and pencil. This time it was Mother. YOU HAD A GOOD TALK WITH YOUR FATHER LAST NITE. THE REASON DAD DID NOT COME TO YOU BEFORE WAS BECAUSE HE HAD NOTHING TO TELL YOU. IT HAD BEEN SO LONG. BUT NOW THERE IS SOMETHING THAT HE CAN DO TOO! WHAT EXCITEMENT WE HAVE HERE TODAY. WE ARE ALL GOING TO WORK HARD TO HELP YOU. I LOVE YOU DEAR.

"What excitement there is here today. We will all help you." I read it over and over again. Yes, they said they'd help, but how? And how could I possibly do it? I seemed so infinitesimally small—like a small birchbark canoe rocking back and forth in a turbulent sea. Back and forth I would go, the sharp waves knocking me over and over then up and down—up and down I went. I seemed to conquer one challenge only to be handed another. Why do I have this responsibility now? Instead let me lie on my back and drift in a calm bay of water with warm sun on my face and clouds floating by to envelop and comfort me. I want to run! to hide! to shout, "NO! NO! I'll do it tomorrow. Not today. Let me be at peace now. Let me rest.' But . . . tomorrow may never be. Tomorrow could end on a busy highway in a mass of torn steel and pools of blood. The now is here! I took the paper, rolled it into the typewriter and started to write again.

Two pages were finished when I heard the noises of the children coming home from schoool. Three o'clock already? My quiet was over for the day. If it wasn't the children it was the doorbell or telephone. How could I possibly get any work done?

I was being totally unrealistic. My job as a mother was too demanding for me now. My writing would have to stop for I could not be everything at once. Maybe next year I would write. Maybe when they were older . . . maybe. I put my writing away.

* * * * *

The weeks went by. I finished the thank you notes. Mother nature had solved some of my problems, for snow had come and covered the leaves and I was gradually getting caught up with some of the more pressing things. A small opening had appeared in my great black cloud of responsibility and sunlight was beginning to filter through. I had a little time now to read. One night I picked up the book, *THE PROPHET,* by the great Lebanese philosopher, Kahlil Gibran. As I fingered through the book I came to his writing on religion, and stopped to read it through. "Who can separate his faith from his actions, or his belief from his occupations?" The words bounced back and forth in my mind. "Who can separate his faith from his actions,...?" I began to slowly realize that this is what I had done. I had separated my faith from my actions. I, who had been so totally committed to share with others what I had learned, had now closed up inside myself. I was afraid. I did not want to write anymore because I was afraid. Fear had taken over—fear that I would not succeed. The fear of failure had set in . . . the fear that I would be laughed at and ridiculed by those who would not understand . . . the fear that my limitations were so great that I could not possibly rise above mediocrity . . . these fears made me a failure before I started. "But what is fear but lack of faith, for if you have faith, you don't have fear." The faith that I had expressed so fervently to others, the faith that had given me such strength during Mac's funeral, I had now closed out. I chose not to use that faith. Instead of meeting the challenges awaiting me I had rejected them. The insidiousness of it oppressed me. How many opportunities would I really be given to express and fulfill my beliefs? How many chances do any of us have in life, only to turn them away? Opportunities to help each other and to grow ourselves avail themselves in many ways every day, and yet more often than not we omit them from our lives. We crawl further into our shell of selfishness. We beg off from possibilities for growth and development and hide behind a fence of false illusion. Then we ask why does our life seem so empty and without meaning?

"I am a failure." I told myself. "I'm a traitor to my conscience and a betrayer of my beliefs. I'm a fraud!" If I had faith, I could do it. If I really had faith, I could write. What had happened to that faith? I had had it before. Maybe I could find it again. I took out pen and paper, said a prayer, and wrote automatically. The cross appeared. It was my Christian guide. I AM YOUR CHRISTIAN. NOW I WANT YOU TO KNOW THAT FAITH IS LIFE. YES, FAITH IS LIFE ITSELF. FOR IF WE DON'T HAVE FAITH, WHY SHOULD WE LIVE? THAT IS HOW IMPORTANT IT IS. IF WE DON'T HAVE FAITH OUR LIFE IS TORN BY INDECISION AND MISUNDERSTANDING. WE DON'T KNOW WHY, NOR CAN WE HAVE ANY MEANING. YES, WE ARE NO MORE THAN A VEGETABLE. WITHOUT FAITH WE ARE LIKE AN EMPTY SUIT OF CLOTHES. FAITH IS OUR REASON FOR BEING. IT IS WHAT MAKES US LIVE. IT GIVES US OUR AIR TO BREATHE AND THE JOY WE HAVE. IT IS WHAT GIVES US JOY AND HAPPINESS. FAITH IS THE FOOD OF OUR LIFE. IT IS THE SUSTENANCE OF OUR EXISTENCE. FOR

NOT TO HAVE FAITH IS NOT TO LIVE. FAITH GIVES US THE STRENGTH TO CLIMB AND SOAR, TO SEARCH AND GROW, TO LOVE AND TO GIVE LOVE. FAITH IS LIFE! FAITH IS IN ALL OF US. IF WE CHOOSE WE CAN ALL HAVE FAITH. IT IS SO EASY, BUT YET VERY HARD FOR SOME. SOME HAVE TO SEARCH AND SEARCH AND STRUGGLE AND STRUGGLE WHILE OTHERS JUST TURN A CORNER AND IT IS THERE. GOD WANTS US ALL TO HAVE FAITH. SO BELIEVE, MY CHILD! BELIEVE THAT HE IS WITH YOU AND IN YOU AND IN EVERYONE. HE SURROUNDS YOU WITH THE BEAUTY OF THE UNIVERSE AND THE MAJESTY OF SOULS THAT OCCUPY IT. HE IS AS CLOSE TO YOU AS YOUR HEART AND YOUR NEIGHBOR! HE IS HERE! GOD IS WITH YOU MY CHILD. BELIEVE AND HE WILL BE YOURS. BELIEVE AND YOU SHALL RECEIVE. BELIEVE AND THE DOOR OF FAITH WILL BE OPEN TO YOU. HE WANTS YOU TO BE HAPPY AND HE WANTS FOR YOU TO MAKE OTHERS HAPPY. THAT IS YOUR MISSION IN LIFE. THAT IS EVERYONE'S MISSION IN LIFE. BELIEVE.

NOW TO BELIEVE IS IMPORTANT, AS I SAID, BUT TO ONLY BELIEVE IS NOT REALLY ENOUGH! WE HAVE TO ACT ON WHAT WE BELIEVE. NOW OF COURSE, CHRIST IS OUR GREATEST TEACHER OF THIS. WE MUST NOT FORGET. IN ORDER TO REALLY HAVE FAITH WE MUST ACT ACCORDING TO OUR BELIEFS. THIS IS THE REAL TEST OF THE FAITH THAT WE HOLD. IF

YOU DON'T ACT YOU WILL REALLY NEVER KNOW
WHAT IT IS LIKE TO HAVE THE BEAUTY OF
FAITH. IT WILL BE STILL AND SILENT IN YOUR
HEART. BUT IF IT IS USED IT WILL BURST FORTH
WITH ALL THE LIFE AND BEAUTY, ENERGY AND
POWER LIKE THE RISING OF THE SUN. THINK OF
THIS POWER THAT WE HAVE INSIDE OF US. SHALL
WE LET IT COME OUT TO LEAD US INTO LIGHT OR
SHALL WE KEEP IT INSIDE SO WE STUMBLE INTO
DARKNESS? LIFE IS BEAUTIFUL, MY CHILD. LIFE,
LIKE THE SUN, CAN BE GOLDEN. MAKE IT GOLDEN
FOR YOU AND FOR THOSE WHO SURROUND
YOU. BE ILLUMINATED BY THE LIGHT THAT IS
WITHIN. SHINE! SHINE! SHINE LIKE THE STARS,
THE MOON, AND THE SUN. SHINE WITH THE FAITH
THAT IS IN YOU. The cross appeared again. He had
signed off. Again, I had my answer. I did believe. Now I
would have to act and would have to write. I took out the
paper and put a sheet into the typewriter. This time I
wouldn't stop. I wouldn't stop until I had finished. For if
you really believe in the power and almighty goodness of
God, you won't say "can't". If you really believe His
greatness is all-encompassing you will say "can". If you
really believe, you won't put the lid on His power, but will
keep yourself completely open to the vast potential that
exists and waits to be tapped. And yet, that is exactly
what I had done. I had put the lid on my faith and had
closed out what I had wanted. I had said, "God, it is true,
you can create miracles, but not in me today. Not now,
thank you. Maybe later." But now, again, I wanted those

miracles. I wanted that help and needed it, but more important I would get it, for I had taken the lid off my closed mind and I was open again. I had removed that lid and had asked for the impossible to become possible. Through believing, you shall receive. As Christ had said, "Whatever you shall ask in prayer, believing, shall come unto you."

I looked outside. The sky was a brilliant blue, contrasting sharply to the sparkling white snow. Tiny crystals of ice glistened and twinkled in the noonday sun. The sun, at its zenith, warmed my face and inspired me, "shine, shine, shine," it seemed to say.

Some pheasants were busy in the back yard eating corn. They were big this year, nice and fat. Out by the pond I saw something move. One, two, three, big orange, bushy tailed foxes were hiding behind a thicket. Maybe it was time for their lunch. For one or two pheasants, life would soon be over. Such is the balance of nature, for there is a time to live and a time to die. My time to live was now! I opened the window and breathed deeply. The fresh cool air permeated my body. I felt young and gloriously alive. What a beautiful day! What a wonderful life!

It was time to rally the forces for a big project was underway. I blew the whistle! A dirty, grubby little face appeared. "Whatcha want, Mom?" Jimmy asked. "We're going to have a meeting in the living room now," I said. In his arms was his ever present box of cars. He took the cars out of the box one by one and "parked" them on the davenport. Each had its proper place. An imaginary network of highways was composed in Jimmy's mind as the davenport became a road and pillows were the bridges. Slowly, he moved the cars back and forth and up and down. Jimmy and his cars were inseparable. I wondered if he would always love cars, as his father had. I wondered if he too, would have a special car some day—a sports car. I wondered . . .

"Mom, can't we have the meeting after dinner? I want to play with Cappi now." Kathleen interrupted my thoughts as her friends bounced and giggled into the living room with her. It seemed to me that Kathleen had been giggling constantly for ten years. What a wonderful way to go through life with a smile and a giggle!

"Mom, Mom, guess what Mom, guess what?"

Mary Susan had come in the front door breathless from her run from the bus. "Mom, I lost my front tooth today. My front tooth came out in school and there was blood all over my desk. It was really neat!"

"Pretty soon you're going to have a shiny new tooth Mary," I said. Losing a tooth always cost me a quarter. The mystery of the tooth fairy had been discovered and now it was strictly a business venture.

Kevin came in and assumed the role as administrator of protocol. "O.K., everyone," he said. "Let's sit in a circle and be quiet."

"Hey Mom," yelled Mike, "can I be president?"

"Not today, Mike. Now we are going to have a very serious discussion. Listen carefully to what I have to tell you. I have decided to write a book. What do you think of that?"

"Neat, Mom," said Mary. "We're just starting to read in school. Can I bring it to school to read?"

"Well, ahh, well, Mary, we'll see." Early in motherhood I had adopted some very sage tactics; whenever in doubt, procrastinate.

"Hey, Mom, that's great! Is Dad going to help you?" Kathleen asked.

"Well yes," I replied. I hoped the neighbors didn't hear that one!

"What's it going to be about?" Kevin wanted to know.

"Well, Kev, it's going to be about all of us. It will be about Daddy and me, you children, God, love, faith, prayer and my automatic writing."

"People are going to think you're nuts, Mom," said Mike.

"Well, we'll just have to take that chance, Mike."

"They'll understand Mike," Kathleen answered. "Adults should be able to understand, if we can."

"I sure hope you're right," I sighed.

"Gosh, it will be fun to write a book." Mary said.

"It won't be just fun, Mary," Kevin added. "It will be a lot of hard work."

"Right Kev, and that's where you children come in. You can help me."

"How can we help you write a book?" asked Mike.

"Well, Mike, you can help me so that I can write the book. You can be quiet when I'm working. That means not to disturb me when I'm writing and to help with more of the work around here." We went through the list of household chores and everyone began to realize that they would all have to help more, for the book had now become a family project.

But it wasn't all work. As the months elapsed we found that we had plenty of time for fun. It was a delightful winter with lots of snow and the moderate temperature not too cold. Kevin, Kathleen, and Mike went skiing every weekend. As their ability improved so did their vitality and appetites—they came home exhausted and hungry. One Saturday, I took everyone skiing. It was Jimmy's first experience and I spent the entire time laughing at him. Every few feet he fell—down into the snow, his chubby body wrapped in layers of clothes, rolling over and over. He would laugh until tears rolled down his face.

It was hard for me to watch the skiers. So many times I had seen Mac come down the same hill, the snow spraying up around him as his body moved gracefully. Jimmy's fun and laughter helped to dispel the pain of this memory.

On the way home he fell asleep in the car exhausted. When we arrived, I put him to bed, and went to the home of some friends for the evening. I returned about midnight and noticed that the light was on in the girls' room. Hurriedly, I went in to see what was the matter. Mary had just awakened. "Jimmy had a picnic, Mom," she said. I looked on the floor and there he was—all curled up on the rug with his blanket held securely in his chubby little fingers. In front of him was a box of potato chips, a jar of marachino cherries, a can of chocolate syrup, a container of whipping cream, and four spoons! Indeed, Jimmy was going to have a picnic! But, after he had gathered all of his goodies, he couldn't wake anyone to have a party so he had fallen asleep on the floor. It had been a big day for a four-year-old skier!

My work continued. Every night the children prayed, "Please God help Mommy with her book." Their prayers were answered, for whenever I needed help, it was there. Friends did typing, and proofreading and helped to take care of the children so I could work. I met a professional writer who offered to do all of my editing and was an enthusiastic source of encouragement.

Then of course, there was the other side . . . The mysterious "other ones", that were always with me. Whenever I couldn't think of what to say I would write automatically and get the answers I needed. Often Mac, but sometimes Mother would write TELL ABOUT THIS OR EXPLAIN THAT. Sometimes I would feel guided to certain books which would help me. But lately a new trick had been taking place. One day I noticed the bell from the kitchen timer was ringing. I had not set the timer, Jimmy was asleep and the children in school. There was no one else in the house . . . strange. I turned it off. Thirty minutes later it went off again. I was suspicious. I went to my paper and pen. HI TWEETIE! Mac wrote. WHEN I HAVE SOMETHING TO TELL YOU I'LL SIGNAL YOU, EITHER THROUGH THIS OR A LIGHT GOING OFF AND ON. From then on, every few weeks the timer would go off. When I heard it ring, I'd say, "O.K. if it's really you, do it again." Then I'd sit in the kitchen and wait. The skeptic was always with me. It always rang again and the information given at that moment was important to either me, the children or the book. Now "they" were reaching me when "they" wanted me. Our communication line was becoming more efficient. Also I learned that my psychic experiences occurred for a reason. They came when they were needed. Whenever I doubted or wondered or questioned, I would receive an answer. It would always come, as most psychic experiences are tied in with the emotional and spiritual needs of the individual. Ordinarily I did my automatic writing sitting up in bed with the paper on a clip board. I was relaxed and comfortable. It was not a scheduled event. I just wrote when I felt like it.

One night I was thinking about how interesting it was that whenever I had the feeling that I should write, I could, and I would usually receive something significant. There would always be a message of some kind. Maybe it would be nothing more than: GO TO SLEEP NOW. YOU'RE TIRED. They were always right. They knew me so well. Then I decided to do some writing. My Christian signed in with his cross symbol. YES, YOU ARE RIGHT. WE ARE WITH YOU TO GUIDE YOU. WE CAN'T FORCE YOU. YOU PAVE THE WAY AND WE LIGHT UP YOUR PATH, TO HELP YOU TO REACH GREATER HEIGHTS. WE WANT TO HELP YOU. IT GIVES US GREAT HAPPINESS. WE KNOW WHEN YOU NEED US BECAUSE WE ARE WITH YOU ALL THE TIME. WE ARE AROUND YOU ALWAYS. NOW, IT IS IMPORTANT ALSO TO KNOW THAT IN ORDER TO ACHIEVE THIS GUIDANCE YOU HAVE TO LEARN

TO BE AWARE OF OUR PRESENCE. YOU HAVE TO
BE STILL AND SILENT AND LET THE VOICE OF
OUR INSPIRATION PENETRATE YOUR MIND. BE
SILENT AND CONTROL YOUR MIND TO LET US BE
HEARD BY YOU. BE STILL AND LET OUR VOICE BE
HEARD. He signed off with his cross. There was no
more. I was learning to develop the ability to hear their
messages. At night, when all was quiet and my mind was
free from thoughts, I could let go and hear the guidance
come through to my inner mind. The messages I received
transcended far beyond limited imagination of the
conscious or subconscious mind. It required a listening.
"Be quiet, Judy," I'd say to myself. "Let them come
through."

There are those who say that this power is part of
another sense of man. It goes far beyond the normal sense
of hearing. It penetrates to an inner awareness, an inner
sensitivity which goes beyond all the other senses. In this
silence we are still able to see, smell, feel, hear, taste and
understand, but all on an intensified level of awareness. It
is through one's listening in meditation that one lifts the
consciousness to this higher level.

While prayer is our direct supplication to God,
meditation is the attuning of ourselves to the spirit so that
God may speak to us.

We know from the history of religions that the
prophets and founders of faiths had all mastered this art of
silence, of meditation. Jesus retired from the crowds to
seek aloneness with God. It is the means by which one can

be renewed by the Spirit overflowing into our lives.

Meditation not only strengthens, guides, and inspires one to greater service to God and man, but it also can help each of us to know ourselves better. As we know ourselves better, we become more humble and more at peace within ourselves. We know that He is with us; watching, loving, forgiving and protecting. A tranquility envelopes us in warmth and security.

Meditation is the key to open the great door of communication. The automatic writing I do is a tangible result of meditation. For me it is evidence which I can read and reread. It has been my key to the door of light. For others who cannot write, meditation can become a great source of meaning. The religions of the East have used it for centuries. For westerners, with our congested, noisy lives, meditation is often difficult to fit into our daily mode of existance. Our style of life has become entrenched with materialism and our habit patterns preoccupied with the noises of television and radio. Yet, many are begging to listen to the sound of silence, thus exploring the many enigmas of life. As Edgar Cayce said in a trance reading on March 2, 1931, "For the time has risen in the earth where men everywhere seek to know more of the mysteries of the mind and the soul."

And the mysteries continued for me. The more I learned, the more questions I had and I knew that I would never stop asking them. There was no going back, and moving forward was becoming more and more exiciting every day.

Is It You Edgar Cayce?

Giving and sharing with others is what makes life full and meaningful. God gives to us, through other people, some of our deepest pleasures and richest joys. I knew that my ability to do automatic writing wasn't meant for me alone, and I soon became aware of a way that I could share it with my friends.

One night in my automatic writing communication from Mac, he suggested I ask his close friend, Reyn, if he would like to communicate with his mother. If he did, Mac would contact her and she could come through in writing to me. I mentioned this to Reyn and he was interested in seeing if it was possible. His mother had died of cancer five years before.

Reyn knew and understood about my automatic writing. He kept his mind open to it, but because he had not experienced anything like it himself, he was doubtful. He wanted proof, as we all did. The day after our talk I had the feeling that I should write. The writing seemed strange this time, and there was no identification made by the communicator. It must be someone new, I thought. WILL YOU PLEASE TELL REYN THAT HE SHOULD NOT WORRY ANY MORE. THAT THINGS WILL BE WORKING WELL FOR HIM NOW. HE IS ON THE RIGHT TRACK. "Who are you?", I mentally asked. MY NAME IS––. I had trouble getting the name. I wasn't sure, but it seemed to be Ruth. TELL HIM THAT I WOULD LIKE TO HELP HIM MORE–THAT I HAVE BEEN WITH HIM. "Who are you?", I asked again. I AM HIS MOTHER. I AM PROUD OF HIM. I LOVE HIM VERY MUCH. TELL HIM THAT I WOULD LIKE TO HELP HIM MORE. THAT HE CAN ASK FOR SOME ANSWER THRU YOU. I CAN HELP HIM. TELL HIM NOT TO BUILD THE STUDIO NOW–NOT A GOOD TIME. TO FIND ANOTHER PLACE TO WORK. TELL MARY I LOVE HER. SHE HAS BEEN A GOOD WIFE AND MOTHER. WORK, MY SON. YOU HAVE SO MUCH TO GIVE THE WORLD. SO MUCH BEAUTY. YOU CAN DO IT. I LOVE YOU.

I thanked her and told her that she could come to me anytime she had something to tell Reyn.

I gave the message to Reyn. He felt that it was real, that it was pertinent to him, but because I knew him and Mary so well, he felt that it could have come from my conscious mind. He could only consider it as a message, to accept it as it was.

There was one major discrepancy in the message: Ruth was not his mother's name! Cancer had damaged her brain, and she had not known herself or anyone else before she died. Could her impaired mentality have carried on into the afterlife and she did not actually know her name? Had a mistake been made either by me or by her? Was the whole thing a puzzle? We didn't know. Reyn said it was nice to believe. He wanted to, but the credibility was lacking because of the name.

"I really have to take the message with a grain of salt, Judy," he told me. "Yet it has forced me to do some concrete thinking about the pros and cons of building the studio. I have made the decision that I would not build. On the day I received the message from you, the contractor called. He was ready to start building that week. I told him I had changed my mind, that I would rent a studio and not build at this time."

I was very upset. Through me, Reyn had been given advice, and he had acted on it. The advice had changed his plans. It could be wrong, completely wrong! Was it right for me to be doing this? Was it right for me to involve myself in other people's lives when I could be making mistakes—mistakes that could be very damaging to them? I was very discouraged. I questioned whether I should continue my writing. It seemed like such a risk to take. I got out my pencil to see what Mac had to say. DO NOT WORRY ABOUT THE NAMES. I DON'T KNOW WHO MADE THE MISTAKE. YOU OR HER. BUT AS I TOLD YOU BEFORE WE WON'T LET YOU MISINTERPRET INFORMATION. DON'T WORRY

ABOUT THE NAME. IT IS NOT IMPORTANT. YOU KNOW IT WAS REYN'S MOTHER. I LOVE YOU.

I was still not satisfied. I was very concerned about her name. It was important to me—very important.

On Monday Reyn started looking for a place to rent. He searched the want ads. He spent a whole day looking at apartments and office space. He needed a place where he could have privacy and plenty of room to work on the many games he had created, the music he wrote, the play he was working on, and his painting.

Tuesday morning I awakened early. I had the feeling I should write. There seemed to be something important coming. I was right. WILL YOU PLEASE TELL REYN THAT HE SHOULD TURN TO PAGE 13 IN THE MORNING PAPER. WALNUT LANE—PAGE 13; I asked her if this was all correct. She replied. YES THAT IS ALL. THANK YOU.

I called Reyn and told him the message. Mary and Reyn were very excited. It looked as if Reyn's apartment search was over. How great! His mother had found a place for him. Hurriedly they searched through the paper. On page 13 there was nothing about Walnut Lane. However, there was an article about the laboratories that had done the extensive tests on his mother's cancer. It was all very puzzling. We were very disturbed. The message had been so specific. What should we do from here? Reyn started pounding the pavement again for a place to work. By Tuesday evening he was very discouraged. He spent the whole day looking at old buildings, grubby stores, and run-down coach houses. He had wandered all over St. Paul.

Late that afternoon, he muttered to himself, "I don't know what I'm supposed to do. I'm confused, bewildered, and discouraged. I've had it! Help me."

At ten o'clock that night I received another message. WILL YOU PLEASE TELL REYN THAT HE SHOULD WORK IN A PLACE THAT IS PLEASANT. WORK IN A NICE PLACE. "Does this mean that he should build his studio?" I asked again. NO! The reply was emphatic, in very large letters. NOT BUILD. She went on. BUT KEEP ON LOOKING. YOU'LL FIND IT SOON. I WANT TO TELL HIM THAT I AM WITH HIM OFTEN BUT HE CAN'T SEE ME. I HAVE HELPED HIM. THAT'S ALL FOR NOW.

I called Reyn and read the message to him. There was silence on his end of the phone. Finally, "Thank you, Judy. I asked for this help, and I got it. I'll go out again tomorrow and look."

The next day he saw an ad for an office in a building that had interested him before. He went to look at it. It was just what he wanted! It was indeed pleasant and very nice! It was perfect for him.

His mother was not through, however, she had more to say. That night a message came again. WILL YOU PLEASE TELL REYN–MORNING PAPER–PAGE 13, WALNUT LANE. THIS IS VERY IMPORTANT FOR HIM. THANK YOU.

"Good heaven," I groaned, "not again! She sure doesn't give up easily. Reyn is going to think I am crazy." I called him and read the message. Again there was silence on the other end of the line. He muttered in exasperation. "Judy, I'd like to tell her, 'Look, Mom, I like the place I've got. I don't want to live on Walnut Lane. I'm a big boy now, and I can find my own place to work. Thanks, but no thanks!' "

"Reyn," I said, "this message is too specific. There has to be something to it. She said it was important to you. Perhaps it has a double meaning."

"I've been going to look at the map for the last two mornings to see if there is a Walnut Lane. I think I'll do it now!" He hung up the phone and I waited. Half an hour later he called back. His voice was excited.

"Judy," he said, "I followed guideline 13 on the map and found a Walnut Street. In Minneapolis it goes right by University Hospital where Mother had her cancer surgery. I know because I visited her there daily. But that's not all. There is also a Walnut Street in St. Paul, and it goes by St. Luke's Hospital where we took Mother after her surgery. It was the last place that she remembered before her brain deteriorated.

Tears of joy came streaming down my face as I realized the impact of the message. Why? Oh why does she have to make it so difficult, so very confusing to us? But Reyn understood. "I'm skeptical, Judy," he said. "I had to be convinced. I needed proof. I am the only one who could possibly appreciate this very personal message. It could not have come from your subconscious mind. It had to be so obscure that only I could comprehend it. It is something that could be shared only by Mother and me."

It was like a puzzle or a game. Only this time it wasn't Reyn who had created it. It was his mother. "Paper–13–Walnut." These were the key pieces. They could be put together by only one person, her son, who had made the many, many trips to the hospital to be at her bedside as she lay dying, and who had the ability to discover the riddle in the message.

I asked him later what the message had really meant to him.

"It was a confirmation of my mother's existence, that she lives on after death and continues her support and love for me as she did in life. The impact of really knowing and believing in a life after death has altered my total concept of living. This experience makes life after death a reality to me and not a hypothetical possibility. It has confirmed what I had wished was true but had only really accepted on a very rational basis. It substantiated what I had perhaps hoped but never thoroughly believed. It was a feeling thing and pervaded my whole being.

"I began to be more aware of the immense opportunities that this state of life has. In this form of life I'm in now I can act out tangibly my growth and development. Whereas I may not have that opportunity when I lack the physical condition of my being. It certainly has been one of the key factors which has led me to believe that the quality of life, what I am and what I'm becoming, is more important than the quantitative aspects of how much, how many, and how fast."

The studio has continued to be "very pleasant and nice" for Reyn. He has been able to work there very well.

The decision he made, with his mother's help, was a good one.

I was pleased with what had happened. No longer was I afraid to ask for other spirits for friends. But I also knew that I could not personally assume the responsibility for the messages which came through me. I was but an instrument, like a telephone carrying the communication between two people. One person was here and the other in the hereafter. As the telephone is not responsible for the messages it carries, neither could I be responsible for the content of what I received. I would have to learn to detach myself from emotional involvement. It wasn't easy, but I knew that if I was to continue to do automatic writing, I would have to. It was up to the receiver of the message to accept or reject, to act on it or not.

I had not heard the last of "Will you please tell Reyn?" messages. A few weeks before Christmas I lay in bed at night, warm and relaxed on the edge of sleep, when I heard in my inner mind, "Will you please tell Reyn?"

Oh no, not now. The voice came back into my mind again, "Will you please tell Reyn?" Sleepily, I got out my pencil and paper and started to write. WOULD YOU PLEASE TELL REYN THAT HE SHOULD NOT WORRY—THAT THINGS ARE GOING WELL FOR HIM—ENJOY MARY AND THE CHILDREN—HAVE FUN AND TRY NEW THINGS. DON'T WORRY. THANK YOU.

Two months later another message came through. As I lay in bed I heard, "Will you please tell Reyn?" I took my pencil and wrote. WILL YOU PLEASE TELL REYN TO BE CAREFUL WITH HIS THROAT AT THIS TIME. THAT IS ALL. THANK YOU. I called Reyn. He was very affected by the message. "I'm going to do some recording this week," he said, "and my voice has to be in good condition. My throat has been bothering me and I have been going to stop smoking. It looks as if I had better do it. Mother is right again.

My mediumship between the here and the hereafter was developing. I began to get requests for spirits from other friends.

One day I was telling a friend about my luck in communicating with spirits. Before I hung up the phone, she asked, "See if you can get Johnny for me, will you?" Johnny was her nine-year-old son, who had died very suddenly in the previous year. He'd been a fun loving, mischievious, active boy. Losing her lively, vibrant child had been very difficult. It was a great shock not only to them but to us. Mac and I had spent many hours with them during the tragedy, and I knew that he would like to "see" Johnny. That night in writing, I asked Mac to see what he could do. The next day I expected that I would be able to communicate with Johnny. I took my pen and paper to see what I could get. HI! TWEETIE. I'M SORRY I CAN'T FIND JOHNNY YET. I SHOULD HAVE HIM SOON. I laughed! Johnny was always great at playing hide and seek. I wondered where he was now.

The next night I tried again. This time I was successful; Mac had found Johnny. The circles began again. Johnny signed in circular writing. He continued. TELL MY MOM NOT TO WORRY—THAT I AM HAPPY HERE. SHE WAS GOOD TO ME AND I CAN DO THINGS FOR HER. WHAT I WANT MOST IS FOR HER TO BELIEVE. IT WILL SOLVE SO MANY PROBLEMS IF SHE UNDERSTANDS ALL OF THIS. TELL HER THAT I AM WITH HER ALOT. I WANT HER TO KNOW THAT SHE IS A VERY GOOD PERSON. SHE IS VERY GOOD! TELL HER THAT I HAD FUN IN LIFE BUT THIS IS REALLY GREAT! I CAN DO SO MUCH MORE. I WANT TO HELP HER MORE. IF SHE BELIEVES, THEN I CAN. ASK HER IF SHE REMEMBERS THE TIME I WALKED ON THE ROOF OF THE HOUSE AND ALMOST FELL OFF. WHAT A NUT I WAS. I WANT YOU TO KNOW THAT YOU WILL BE HAPPY IF YOU WILL UNDERSTAND THIS. KEEP ON TRYING. MOM AND DAD I LOVE YOU.

I called Johnny's mother. We both cried as I read the message. "Yes," she said. "I do remember his walking on the roof of the house. It was no little accomplishment because it was a two story house. Nothing was too great a challenge for Johnny." He had been a beautiful memory but now he had come alive again in words, if not in body.

Johnny had exhausted me. I took a long nap but still felt weak when I awoke. I knew that spirits utilized my energy for the writing, but I had never felt so exhausted as I did this time. I did not feel this way with Mac or Mother. I don't know what made the difference. Perhaps older spirits knew how to better utilize this energy than Johnny did.

Johnny returned to me quite unexpectedly a few months later. As I took up my pen to write, a message came. MY NAME IS JOHNNY. WILL YOU PLEASE TELL MY PARENTS THAT I WANT THEM TO BE HAPPY. I LOVE THEM. THANK YOU. That was all. It was very simple but made me feel warm and happy . . . I hope Johnny will come back again.

My life was very busy with writing, managing the household, caring for the children, and adjusting to the role of a single woman in the married society that surrounded me. My body was still very tired from the shock of Mac's death and the increasing burdens on it. Usually after dinner I would go to my bedroom and read. It was warm and cozy in my room with the children bouncing in and out. They always had something to ask me, something to talk about, something to share. The living room seemed cold and lonely to me because Mac's absence was most conspicuous there. His reading chair was empty and the guitar that had always been next to it was gone. Never again would he play "Five Hundred Miles." It was the first song he learned and we kidded him about playing it so often. "Five hundred times we've heard 'Five Hundred Miles'!"

The smell in the living room was different too. The aroma of his pipe that I liked so much, was gone. The smoky haze that had filled the room at night and lasted throughout the next day was not there. That warm, protecting, secure scent was no longer with us. The "good smokers" that he always lost were now gone for good. The ash tray beside his chair was empty.

I stayed out of the living room. Instead I would curl up in bed and read about the world of the occult. I wanted to know everything that I could about psychic phenomena.

Edgar Cayce was my favorite subject. His medical treatments fascinated me. To our sophisticated world many of them seemed absurd, but they worked, and how else could they be judged? Healing and helping people when they are sick is a blessed gift and one which I had always valued highly. Now I read with amazement about this astonishing man, who is more widely known now than when he was alive. A foundation called the Association of Research and Enlightenment has been formed to compile and distribute all of the information accumulated during his lifetime. People all over the world are reading and studying the knowledge that has come through him as he lay in a trance.

One night I was re-reading *The Other Side,* by Bishop Pike. The book told of his participation in a seance in an effort to communicate with his son, Jim. During the seance Edgar Cayce said through the medium, "I want to help you develop spiritual healing." He then referred Pike to books that he wanted him to read. I was impressed that Cayce was still "active" on the earth plane. In death as in life he was still helping others.

My neighbor, Carol, called the next day. She was very worried about her husband Jack, who had been in the hospital for eight days with torn muscles in his leg. The Doctor felt it would take a long time for the swelling to be reduced. He was out of the hospital now, but the leg was still very swollen and uncomfortable. I hung up the phone and started to do some thinking. Edgar Cayce would know what to do about this case. He would have some very different solution that the doctors would not have thought about. I realized what I had to do. I would ask for Edgar Cayce to come through in automatic writing. Again, the courage of my convictions was being tested. Again, I would have to take the "lid off" of the powers of God and ask for the impossible. Again, I would have to say, "I can't do it, God, but You can. Help me to help someone else." I was shooting for the moon, and I knew it. That night in my automatic writing, I asked Mac to get me Edgar Cayce. "That will keep Mac busy," I chuckled, as I fell asleep.

The next night I was hopeful but scared, as I began to write. I didn't want to be disappointed. I took a deep breath of air and put my pencil down. Circles began to form again. I had someone new. I AM EDGAR CAYCE. I WOULD LIKE TO HELP YOU. I told him about Jack and where he lived. I WILL LOOK INTO IT FOR YOU, was the message I got. The pencil stopped. A few minutes later the pencil began to move again. I HAVE HIM NOW. HIS LEG HAS BEEN INJURED AND HE HAS CIRCULATION PROBLEMS. I WOULD ADVISE THAT HE USE COMPRESSES IN THE MORNING AND NITE. THESE COMPRESSES SHOULD BE MADE OF WITCH HAZEL. This seemed so strange to me that I asked him to repeat it. WITCH HAZEL came again in

writing composed of many circles. He went on, A
SOLUTION OF THIS COMBINED WITH WATER 2 TO
1. NOW THIS SHOULD BE DONE EVERY MORNING
AND NITE FOR FIFTEEN MINUTES. HE SHOULD
NOT SMOKE AND HAVE PLENTY OF REST. HE
SHOULD BE VERY CAREFUL NOT TO OVERDO. HE
SHOULD HAVE PLENTY OF REST, EAT A LOT OF
VEGETABLES, AND NOT TOO MUCH MEAT. THE
LEG SHOULD NOT BE USED EXCEPT WHEN
NECESSARY. HE SHOULD REST A LOT. BE SURE
TO DO THE COMPRESSES. THESE ARE VERY
IMPORTANT FOR HIM. I WILL HELP YOU AGAIN. I
thanked him. YOU'RE WELCOME. EDGAR
CAYCE. I looked in wide-eyed amazement as my hand
moved to form a very distinctive signature as he signed off.

I called Carol and Jack and asked them to come over.
Without any words I handed them the paper. We all read
and reread the message many times. Had the impossible
become possible? Was this message really from Edgar
Cayce? We had no way of knowing. The one thing that I
was sure of was that this information could have never
come from my conscious or subconscious mind. This
information simply was not within me. Handing out
medical information was a serious business and something
that I didn't want to tamper with. Never in my wildest
moment could I have conjured up such advice for an
injured leg.

The message was for Jack to use as he wished. He
bought the Witch Hazel and made the compresses. The
swelling did go down. Was this another miracle or merely

coincidence? We did not know. The curative powers of Witch Hazel had no correlation with the aroma it gave off. Jack's leg really smelled!

My mind jumped back and forth between belief and disbelief. How could it be that I was really communicating with Edgar Cayce? It seemed so fantastic, so amazing that I couldn't believe it. "But just a minute Judy," the still voice inside me said. "Remember what you said about faith? Remember what you said about taking the 'lid off' the powers of God and letting him work through you?" Yes, of course it is possible. There are absolutely no limits to the powers of God. Yes, it could be another miracle in my life. It could be true.

I decided to talk to Mac. Is it really true? I asked. YES, TWEETIE, IT IS REALLY EDGAR CAYCE. HE CAME TO YOU BECAUSE HE WANTS TO HELP YOU AND MANY OTHERS. BELIEVE. IT IS TRUE. I LOVE YOU.

Time solves many problems. Perhaps time will give me the answers that I need. I will have to be patient and use Edgar Cayce when I need him. Maybe someday I will know if it is really he.

Edgar Cayce, in the hereafter, could not sew up the injuries of my children, but I learned that he could help me with many of their problems.

Kevin's injured leg was causing him trouble. Occasionally the muscle would spasm and he would be in misery. One day he asked me to contact Cayce about his leg. It was a simple request by my son, who believed. I wished that I had the faith of a child. Nevertheless, I asked

Mac for Edgar Cayce. He came right through without any waiting. I AM EDGAR CAYCE. CAN I HELP YOU. I told him about Kevin. HE NEEDS HOT COMPRESSES OF WITCH HAZEL APPLIED EVERY HOUR FOR TEN MINUTES AND GENTLE MASSAGE. I asked, "Can he use the leg?" EXERCISE WILL BE ALL RIGHT. YES, IT WILL HELP TO STRETCH THE MUSCLE. HEAT AT NIGHT WILL BE GOOD. I asked him if he should stay home from school the next day. NO, HE WILL BE BETTER. KNOW THAT WE ARE WITH YOU AND ARE HELPING YOU. EDGAR CAYCE.

I thanked him and went to the store and bought some Witch Hazel. We followed Cayce's instructions. They worked. I was becoming a believer. I had a doctor in my hand and I didn't even get a bill!

Kevin became a good candidate on which to "test" Edgar Cayce. Something was always happening to him. One Saturday night he came home from a neighbors at about 10:30. He had eaten half a filbert kernel and had an allergic reaction to it. His eyes were watering; his nose was congested; his skin was red and blotchy; and he itched severely from hives. I didn't want to call a doctor so late on a Saturday night, so I decided to wait for an hour to see what would happen. If he got worse or had trouble breathing I was prepared to rush him to the hospital. An hour passed. He wasn't any worse but he wasn't any better either. He was very worried and becoming frantic from the discomfort.

"Mom, will you please ask Edgar Cayce for some help?" he begged of me.

"Kevin, Edgar Cayce would probably have me chop up some roots from the garden to give to you." I answered.

"Please Mom!" He asked.

I gave in but first I tried to prejudge the situation to see what I would do. The only thing that I could think to use was calamine lotion to alleviate the itching. This would be very little help, if any. I got out my paper and pencil to see what Edgar had to say. THIS IS EDGAR CAYCE. I explained the situation. YES. NOW IT WILL TAKE A LITTLE WHILE TO CLEAR THIS UP. FOR NOW HE SHOULD TRY TO SLEEP. BY MORNING HE WILL BE BETTER. I told him that Kevin wanted to take a bath. The answer was NO HOT WATER—YOU COULD TRY SOME ALCOHOL. I asked him to repeat the last word. ALCOHOL came again in shaky letters. NOW HE WILL BE ALL RIGHT. I thanked him. YOU'RE WELCOME, EDGAR CAYCE. The signature was the same every time.

I had some rubbing alcohol, and began to sponge Kevin's hot, red skin with it. I poured it into a basin to soak his itchy feet and hands. As the alcohol touched his skin, the redness and heat left and the itching went away. In twenty minutes he was greatly relieved and fell asleep. The next morning Kevin woke rested and comfortable. Dr. Cayce had done it again! Kevin accepted it as a matter of course. I was still in awe.

Mary Susan seemed listless, as she picked at her food on Thanksgiving. After dinner she vomited. She had a headache and a temperature of 101. I groaned, "It looks as if we have the flu again." When one of the children in a large family gets the flu, the others usually do too. Flu was something I didn't look forward to. Kevin suggested that I contact Edgar Cayce for advice. It seemed rather ridiculous to me. I had taken care of children with the flu many times. Nevertheless, I decided to see what Cayce would say. I took my paper and pen and began to write. I AM EDGAR CAYCE. I told him about Mary. I HAVE HER. SHE SEEMS TO HAVE AN INFECTION IN HER THROAT. I WOULD SUGGEST THAT YOU APPLY WARM COMPRESSES TO HER NECK. BED REST, AND LOTS TO DRINK. Thank you, I said. He responded with YOU'RE WELCOME, and his now familiar signature.

A throat infection. I thought about that for awhile. She didn't seem to have anything wrong with her throat. He must be wrong. The next morning Mary woke up, complaining of a very sore throat. Edgar Cayce was not wrong. I followed his advice. It helped.

As I said my prayers of thanks for this gift of communication I began to ponder how I could help others by using Edgar Cayce. It was a gift that I wanted to share. But how? I had so few believers to work with. Perhaps Edgar Cayce could help me. He had the same problem in his life. I asked for him the next night. He signed in right away. THIS IS EDGAR CAYCE. MY CHILD, THERE IS SOMETHING VERY IMPORTANT FOR YOU TO KNOW. YOU MUST REMEMBER THAT THE GIFTS YOU HAVE BEEN GIVEN HAVE GREAT

OBLIGATIONS TO THEM. YOU MUST NOT FORGET THAT YOU MUST USE THEM TO ENRICH OTHER PEOPLE'S LIVES. YOU MUST NOT USE THEM FOR SELFISH GOALS. NOW IF YOU WISH TO HEAL PEOPLE YOU WILL BE ABLE TO DO SO AS I WILL BE HAPPY TO HELP YOU. PEOPLE WILL BELIEVE IN YOU MORE AND MORE IF YOU ARE SINCERE IN YOUR EFFORTS AND DESIRE TO HELP. THEY WILL SEE THE RESULTS AND COME TO YOU BUT IT DOES TAKE TIME. I KNOW. BELIEVE IN YOURSELF AND YOUR GIFTS. NEVER FORGET THAT YOU HAVE TAPPED THE GOD POWER IN YOU. IT IS VERY BEAUTIFUL AND POWERFUL AND THE MORE IT IS USED WELL, THE MORE YOU WILL RECEIVE. YOU ARE DOING VERY WELL NOW. BE PATIENT MY CHILD. YOU HAVE MANY MANY GIFTS. BE PATIENT. YOU HAVE BEEN GIVEN MUCH. ENJOY IT AND IT WILL GROW. YOU NEED MORE REST SO BE SURE TO ELIMINATE ALL OF THE THINGS THAT ARE UNIMPORTANT TO YOU. JUST REMEMBER THAT WHAT YOU ARE DOING TAKES ENERGY. YOUR PHYSICAL CONDITION IS IMPORTANT. I WILL HELP YOU ANY TIME YOU ASK. IT IS MY JOB TO HELP YOU. DO NOT HESITATE. IT IS MY JOY TO HELP YOU WITH ANYTHING I CAN.

Yes, he was right. Be patient, get rest, and things will happen. It was difficult for me to be patient. My delight about my new communicator was something I wanted to share with the whole world. But I couldn't. If I was to help anyone, it would have to be myself first. For if I didn't take care of myself I wouldn't be able to do anything. I had to take it slow.

Gradually things did begin to happen. Friends came to me with requests to ask for advice from Cayce. They came from people all over the city. As Cayce had said, IT IS MY JOY TO HELP YOU. So it was also *my* joy to help others. For me, there could be no greater joy.

I couldn't worry about whether people used the information I got or whether it worked. I was the instrument, and if the instrument was going to work well, it had to remain detached. There were times when I went to our doctor for treatment for the children. Antibiotics had come into use since Cayce's lifetime. They were powerful and effective in combating infection, and I didn't hesitate to use them when the children were very sick. Modern medicine has many answers which didn't exist in Cayce's day. I tried to be realistic about his advice. Yet we all know that medical science is not perfect. There are too many unanswered questions, too many uncured diseases, and too many unsolved problems. Cayce had many answers.

One morning I received a call from a friend. His voice was tense and worried. He told me his 19-year-old daughter was in critical condition. She was hospitalized with a bladder infection. If she didn't improve in a few hours, the doctors would have to perform major surgery, which could be very dangerous for her.

I hung up the phone. I then called the members of my prayer group and asked them to pray hard for her all day. Then I went to my bedroom to meditate on what I could do for her. I closed off my mind from all outside thoughts and asked for an answer. "Do not operate. Do not operate. Do not operate. Do not operate." Those words rushed through my head. I knew it was Cayce communicating with me. I got out my pencil and paper to find out what he had to tell me. I AM EDGAR CAYCE. THIS GIRL DOES NOT NEED AN OPERATION. THEY MUST USE HOT COMPRESSES OF BOOKS BOOKS. I couldn't figure it out. It didn't make sense. I was confused. I tried to completely close out my own thoughts, to be receptive to Cayce. Then, in very shaky letters came, WILL YOU PLEASE LET ME SAY IT? BOOK ON THE BOTTOM SHELF IN YOUR ROOM. I went to the night table where I had some books, one of which was on health herbs. It was the only book in the stack that I thought Cayce might want. I picked it up. Then I took my paper and pencil again. YES, THIS SHOULD HAVE IT. My mind was racing. It was so bewildering. What should I do now? I looked through the index. What should I look for? Infections? No, not listed, but inflamations were: "Inflamations, herbs for treatment of, page 354." I turned to page 354. Listed there were about 40 different herbs. What should I do now? I closed my eyes and put my pencil on the page. Back and forth the pencil went until I noticed it moving stronger and heavier. I opened my eyes and saw that the pencil had underlined in dark writing many times, Golden Seal. I put the book down and started writing again. YES, GOLDEN SEAL POULTICES EVERY HOUR FOR TEN MINUTES

WITH HOT COMPRESSES IN BETWEEN. PLENTY OF
LIQUIDS. I thanked him. YOU'RE WELCOME. EDGAR
CAYCE.

I went back to the herb book to read about Golden
Seal.

> "This is one of the most wonderful remedies in
> the entire plant kingdom. When it is considered all
> that can be accomplished by its use, and what it
> actually will do, it does seem like a real cure-all. It is
> especially effective in all Catarrhal conditions whether
> of the stomach, bladder, or where there is a lining of
> the mucous membrane. It kills poisons."

I tried to call my friend to give him the information
but I couldn't reach him. I visualized him carrying a
package of herbs into the hospital and trying to convince
the doctor to use them, what a laugh! How could he
possibly utilize this treatment in the hospital? I didn't
know, but at least I had to tell him. It was evening before I
reached him. "She's out of danger now," he said. "She
won't need the operation." I was so relieved. Even though
we lost an opportunity to use one of Cayce's treatments, I
knew there would be more in the future, and I was firm in
my belief that Cayce was with me to give help when he
was needed.

Another friend had been following my experiences
with automatic writing with much interest. She decided
to try to write. Phyllis was able to communicate,
but not as successfully as I. She asked me if I could
help her with some information about her health. I in turn

asked Edgar Cayce, who told me that she should get more rest and not work so hard. She began to feel worse. It was obvious that she needed corrective surgery. Edgar Cayce came through to her one night when she was doing some automatic writing. YOU MUST HAVE SURGERY. YOU NEED OPERATION AS SOON AS POSSIBLE. EDGAR CAYCE. We were amazed to see that the signature that she had received from Cayce was very similar to mine!

Several weeks later she had the operation. While recuperating at home one day, she did some automatic writing. She called me afterwards. "Judy," she said, "I seem to have Edgar Cayce coming through in my automatic writing, but it doesn't seem to make any sense. I just get two words. Would you mind checking with him to see if you can figure it out? I got out my pen and paper and began to write. I HAVE COME TO HELP YOU MY CHILD. YES, I AM EDGAR CAYCE. I told him about Phyllis. YES, I WANTED HER TO KNOW THAT THE BRACE IS FOR SUPPORTING HER BACK. SHE COULD USE THAT NOW. SHE CAN FIND THIS OUT THRU HER DOCTOR. I asked him about the other word. YES—PACKS OF MAGNESIUM CAN HELP HER. SHE CAN LOOK INTO THIS.

Phyllis did look into it. The brace and the treatment were helpful. Cayce had come through again.

Another one of my guides also came to Phyllis. She called me one night. "I've been writing, and when I looked at the paper, my pen had formed a strange sign. It looks like two triangles put together, point to point, like a butterfly. After that came the message. I WILL HELP

TAKE CARE OF YOU." "That sounds like my protection guide," I replied. He must be working overtime. The next day I went to see her. Phyllis had never seen mine before but her symbol was the same.

A woman who'd had a great deal of experience in the occult and in communicating with spirits told me one day to ask for my own guide. I didn't quite understand. "I have many guides. What do you mean by my own guide?" I asked.

"The spirits with which you have been communicating are either the loved ones you knew on earth or those which have come to help you with something special, such as the writing you are doing. But everyone has a guide which has been with him since birth, guiding him throughout life. These guides are highly trained and can help you in many ways in which the spirits who have just come over can't. You should really ask to communicate with your own particular guide. It will be very important to you."

Why not? I thought. Perhaps I would get my real guardian angel. It had never occurred to me that I did have a special guide.

I didn't quite know what to do or where to begin. So I prayed. After praying the Lords Prayer, I asked God to bring me to my guide. I began to write.

I AM DR. CARVER. NOW PLEASE LISTEN TO ME CAREFULLY. I HAVE BEEN WITH YOU ALL OF YOUR LIFE. I SAW YOU AS THE DAUGHTER I NEVER HAD. YOU WERE MY CHILD—THAT'S WHY I

GUIDED YOU. I'M HAPPY TO HELP YOU AS BY HELPING YOU I HELP MYSELF TOO! THE REASON THAT I DIDN'T COME TO YOU BEFORE IN YOUR WRITING IS BECAUSE YOU WOULD HAVE BEEN AFRAID OF A SPIRIT THAT YOU DIDN'T KNOW. I HAD TO WAIT UNTIL YOU WERE READY TO KNOW ABOUT ME. I WAS THE ONE THAT TOLD YOU WHEN YOUR MOTHER WOULD DIE. I WAS THE ONE THAT PRODDED YOU TO DO THE READING YOU DID WHICH PREPARED YOU FOR WHAT YOU ARE DOING NOW. I WAS THE ONE THAT GAVE YOU THE WARNINGS OF YOUR HUSBAND'S DEATH. I HAVE BEEN WITH YOU ALL ALONG, HELPING AND GUIDING YOU. NOW THAT WE ARE ABLE TO COMMUNICATE BETTER, I WILL BE ABLE TO HELP YOU MORE.

NOW, I MUST EXPLAIN TO YOU THAT I AM NOT A MEDICAL DOCTOR. THAT IS A TITLE THAT WE RECEIVE HERE BECAUSE OF THE TRAINING WE GO THROUGH. IT IS WHAT YOU MIGHT CALL AN ADVANCED DEGREE. WE CAN DO MANY THINGS AND BECAUSE I HAVE BEEN WITH YOU SO MUCH, I KNOW YOU BETTER THAN ANYONE ON EARTH. NOW IT IS TRUE THAT EVERYONE ON EARTH HAS A SPIRIT GUIDE LIKE ME. YES, IT IS TRUE! IF YOU WANT TO CALL US ANGELS, GUIDES, GOD OR GOD POWER, IT IS ALL THE SAME. WE ARE WHAT PROVIDES THAT INSIGHT OR INTUITION FOR PEOPLE. WE CAN GUIDE THROUGH MANY WAYS. YOU DO IT THROUGH YOUR

198198

WRITING BUT OTHERS RECEIVE THEIR GUIDANCE THROUGH FEELINGS. MANY TIMES WE CAN COME THRU TO PEOPLE WHEN THEY ARE DREAMING. IT IS IMPORTANT THAT PEOPLE KNOW THAT THEY DO HAVE THIS EXTRA HELP WHEN THEY NEED IT. IF PEOPLE CAN BECOME MORE AWARE OF THIS, THEY WILL LEARN TO RECOGNIZE IT AND WE WILL BE ABLE TO HELP MORE EFFECTIVELY. RELIGIONS OFTEN CALL THIS GRACE. IT IS A GOOD WORD BUT NOT UNDERSTOOD AS IT REALLY SHOULD BE. GOD SENDS US TO HELP YOU MY CHILD. THRU GOD WE ARE ABLE TO HELP YOU. ASK AND YOU SHALL RECEIVE THE GRACE AND BEAUTY AND GUIDANCE IN YOUR LIFE. ASK AND YOU SHALL RECEIVE. THAT IS ALL FOR NOW. I WILL COME AGAIN.

I said a prayer of thanks and read again what I had written. Yes, of course, I thought. It all makes sense. This message added to the image I had of a very loving and helpful God. But why, oh why do we humans have to make it so hard for ourselves? Why do we close off the help we have coming to us and insist on struggling through our own personal hells alone? Why, oh why, can't we all learn to open ourselves up to the powers of God? Why don't we learn to tap this tremendous source of power within ourselves?

I read again. ASK AND YOU SHALL RECEIVE. Perhaps, I thought, it is simply because we don't ask.

Doubt would creep into my mind periodically about the authenticity of my messages from Edgar Cayce. Could it really be true? About a month had passed without my communicating with him. I had been very busy and had no need for his advice. One night I decided to write. I had no question to ask. I just thought I would see who came through. IT IS I, MY CHILD, EDGAR CAYCE. YES, I HAVEN'T BEEN WITH YOU FOR AWHILE BUT I JUST WANTED TO ASSURE YOU THAT I AM STILL WAITING FOR YOU TO CALL. EDGAR CAYCE. The doubt was still in my mind. I left my hand on the paper. Another spirit was coming. MY NAME IS DOCTOR CARVER. YES, MY CHILD IT IS EDGAR CAYCE. My symbol for honesty appeared. THIS IS HONESTY. YES, IT IS EDGAR CAYCE.

I wanted to believe that it was Edgar Cayce communicating with me. Yet, how could I not doubt? My mind told me to probe and question everything. My basic senses could not guide me for there was no tangible way that I could prove it.

Instead I had to judge the messages from him by the way they worked. Time and time again they provided good advice that had proved helpful to many people. Yes, they had worked.

Maybe someday I will really know, Edgar Cayce, if it is you. Perhaps that day will not be in the here but in the hereafter. For now, I can only thank God for what has come to me. It works!

Believe My Child

The wonders of God continue to unfold around me. I am still surprised at, amazed by, confused with and doubtful of the psychic experiences that occur. The simple, uncluttered minds of my children accept these happenings readily, while I question and often reject. I ask myself whether I have benefited from the years of education I've had or whether I'm a victim of an educational system that discourages us from investigating all of the mysteries and the potentials of life.

The children nudge me back into the reality of the spiritual life around us. As we sat one evening and talked in the living room, one of the lights blinked off an on. I checked the bulb. It was screwed in tightly. I tried the bulb in another outlet. It worked well. I put the bulb back into its socket and ignored it. The blinking continued.

Finally Kathleen said, "Why don't you see what Daddy wants?"

When she left the room to get paper and pencil for me the blinking stopped. I wrote. It was Mac. I LOVE YOU. I AM HAPPY FOR YOU. EVERYTHING WILL BE ALL RIGHT. I AM WITH YOU.

Later that evening a friend who had been a great help to me and the children, came to visit. While we sat and talked, a different light began to blink. Slowly it would dim: off and on. I picked up the paper again to write. This time it was a message for my friend. I AM VERY GRATEFUL, ANDY, FOR THE HELP AND HAPPINESS YOU HAVE GIVEN MY FAMILY. THANK YOU. The spirit of Mac continued to be with us. "Golly," Mary said, "Daddy's here again. Aren't we lucky?"

Our society has a fear and distrust of the spiritual world. The Salem witch burnings of our country's early years and the cult of demon worshippers today cause alarm to many. "Stay away from spirits," many people warn. But why? Spiritual experiences can have value and are expressed in many different ways. Sometimes it is through the happy voice of Jimmy as he says, "Daddy's here with us. He helps. We can't see him though." The other children too, have learned not to fear death and know that the love of their father continues to be with them. It is also through me, who feels peace in knowing that I have a big job to do and that I will have help in doing it. But the circle of light which has awakened me has spread further for many people have lived through these experiences with me. Their new understanding of the power and beauty of God has enriched their lives, with meaning and a sense of real purpose.

A close friend suddenly discovered she had to have a breast removed to stop the spread of cancer. It was a shock to her, her husband, and their four young children. I went to visit her in the hospital shortly after the operation. She sat up in bed. There was a smile on her face and a sparkle in her eyes. "Judy," she beamed, "I could never have handled this a year ago, but since Mac's death and your experiences, I understand more about the obstacles in life. I've always had it soft," she said. "Things have come easily for me. I'd decided lately that I wanted to go back to school, to further my education in psychology. I wanted to do what I could to help young people with their problems. It troubled me that I had never had any real hurdles to deal with in my own life, and I realized that it would be difficult for me to relate to the problems of others. Then I had cancer. The doctor has said my recovery is certain and I'm sure he is right. But more than that, I have experienced a challenge that I have mentally and physically overcome, not only through myself but also by the powers of God and the love of many friends." Her room was filled with flowers. Her friends had remembered her. They also had fed and helped her family while she was hospitalized. "I would have felt obligated to my friends before, but now I realize that we all have to give and share in this life, and it would be wrong for me to deny them the gift of giving. Now I can use my experience to help others too! I can show them that we can get through the obstacles that confront us with courage and help from God."

As I turned to say good-bye, she had a cheery smile on her face. I knew that she was using what had happened to her to grow and to enrich her life and the lives of many others. What could have been an oppressing, devastating, negative situation, had been turned into a positive learning experience.

Love that we express through giving and helping others grows. The good that we do continues; nothing good is ever lost. Just before his death, Mac struggled to find a way to help the starving children of Biafara. The students at Macalester College remembered his work. They staged a 72 hour rock music concert, in memory of him, for the aid of Biafara relief.

The children and I sat in the chapel after the exhausted performers were finished. We listened to the message from the Rev. Larry Dare:

"We are here to do more than receive and dedicate the offering of these hours of effort and some gifts of money for tne relief of human suffering across the world.

"We are here to do more than remember the life, joy, and concern of a man, Jim McCarthy, who cared and worked in .ove for his brother.

"We are here to celebrate life, and to rejoice in freedom, which is the substance of life. The memory of Jim is but the focal point, or the windows, by which we can see life and know what real freedom means.

"Life appears—when men have the basic sustenance of living and can break loose from the daily agony of sheer survival.

"Life appears—when a man, like Jim McCarthy, can take hold of it, shake it, make it dance, pull some purpose of his own from it, know and express both its depths and heights in joyous concern with his brother.

"Life appears—when men break through their separations and join together in the circle games of human existence, sharing the common needs, joys and pains.

"And freedom is not different from life.

"Like life itself, freedom is a doing, as well as a being.

"Like life itself, freedom is never total. It is always seeking, always becoming.

"Like life itself, freedom can never stay alone. It must always move toward the other, where alone the self is known and completed.

"Freedom appears—where men can think and eat, dream and create; where food and clothing and shelter are the floor of life and not its ceiling.

"Freedom appears—where a man emerges from the purely conventional, the routine, and the self-imprisonment to move loose-jointedly to the music of this world and his own soul.

"Freedom appears—where men can leap over the barriers of alleged necessity, of iron-clad ideology, and even of the supposedly natural—to become men together; suffering, organizing, rejoicing, and celebrating.

"It is thus that our small help to brothers in a distant place gains its only meaning and fulfillment.

"It is thus that a free, vital, striving man, though he were dead, still lives.

"Thus life emerges out of death."

Tears ran down my face. My throat tightened, choking me with emotion, as I thanked them in behalf of a man who was not forgotten and who still lives in memory and spirit with us.

The Biafara of yesterday becomes the who-knows-what crisis of tomorrow. The wars continue. Man has not yet learned to solve his problems without killing. Warfare remains a tool of our existence and fighting, a way of life. War begets more war.

As mankind persists to struggle and strive, to grow and build, it also fragments and destroys with its opposing idealogies. Communism, fascism, and democracy all promise a better world. Within each are positive elements but instead of uniting their common positive values, they conflict until the world burns from the heat of battle and scourges itself with the red blood of defeat. Every thinking man becomes disillusioned by having to make the choice between the political movements, which leave us desperately wanting something larger, finer and better for mankind. At the present rate of increase, the world's population will number six billion people by the year 2000. What kind of a world awaits a baby being born into the new century? Will he be born only to be instantly fitted with a gas mask so that he won't have to breathe the deadly, polluted air? Will he be able to enjoy the beauty of our natural resources, or will the earth have become a mass of concrete and steel to house its bulging humanity? Will he be regarded as an individual or will he become just a number in a total computer system of inputs and readouts? Will our streams and rivers be immense cesspools of the waste products of man? Will all of our trees be defoliated as in Vietnam? Will the world that man has despoiled and prostituted become so repugnant to him that he chooses the barren wasteland of the moon or a gyrating space station in orbit as his vacation spot?

Have the scientists become the heroes of our time? The atom has been split. With this enormous energy man can power the earth—or destroy it. Deadly smallpox and crippling polio have become diseases of the past; yet now the number one killer is heart disease, aggravated by the tensions, pressures, and stress of a demanding society. The world is a neighborhood because jet travel brings the continents hours closer for pleasurable communication or minutes away for deadly missile destruction. Most Americans enjoy the comfort and convenience of owning their own automobiles, but the price we pay is highways belching forth noxious gases, and ribbons of concrete cutting into the beauty of our countryside, while the shining chrome products of Detroit's ingenuity jam together, horns blasting, wheels shrieking, making us want to scream, "Damn the man that invented the wheel!"

No, science and technology have not solved all of our problems. In eliminating some, others have been created. The vicious cycle of man's dilemma continues to continue. The generation gap widens. Many parents are content with the material success they have achieved with hard work. Their work week shortens, making more leisure time available and higher wages make luxuries available for almost everyone. "Don't you see?" their children demand, "We want the black man to have equal opportunities too. We don't want to go to war and kill and be killed!" Young and old shake their heads at each other in misunderstanding. Some "cop-out". In their troubled world they turn to drugs to pleasure their senses or to hopefully expand their consciousness to find significance to their lives. Others pursue hedonistic pleasures only to find that after the thrill is gone, the emptiness remains within them.

Should we look to the church for answers? Its membership is dropping in numbers never before witnessed. Our youth are turning away. The church's schools are closing their doors. Is it because people are losing their religion or is it because there are those who are unable to find religion inside the church? "Love thy neighbor," Christ said. "As long as he is white," many answer. "Thou shalt not kill." "Unless it's in another country," others respond. Should not the church be the moral guidelight of our society? Should it not act on the commandments it teaches? The hypocrisy, the contradictions that many people now see within its doors turns them away. The youth of today are inspired by the challenges of our times. They have been educated to think and act according to their consciences. Many have given up trying to relate to structures that are tied to the traditions, rules, and customs of a multi-standard past. Members of the "now" generation express themselves differently from their fathers. Their language is new. Their music is their own. Their long, loosely hanging hair and brightly styled clothes reveal a freedom and individuality that seem strange and threatening to their parents and grandparents.

Students march for miles to draw attention to their causes and to express their feelings. "Stop the War." "We Don't Want to Kill." "Love Not War" the signs read. Their hair is often long and shaggy and their clothes messy and dirty, as they protest the clean antiseptic sterile society that has given them another war to fight and more people to kill. Could Nazi Germany have happened if their youth had been the vocal, active young people that we have in America today? Was there not another who walked the streets many centuries ago, whose hair was long and whose clothes hung loosely down to his bare feet as He preached love and peace? Is Christ locked inside the church or is He walking with our young down the roads of protest?

Can the church become alive, vibrant, relevant to our contemporary world? Can it be the necessary moral guide and activator of our troubled society? Many youth of today answer "no" and the established churches and structured religions give way to the Jesus revolution that is sweeping the country today revealing a more accessible and personal Christ. The rockgroups call Him Superstar. On the beach in California He guides the surfers. Drug users go to Him for help. Communes form to know Him better and the Pentecostal fervor builds up interspersing itself throughout all of formal religions. There appears to be a revival of religion everywhere. Even though the form the "Now" generation's faith takes may seem strange to the traditionally oriented, being "turned on" to Jesus, whether it be by mystical, emotional experiences or intellectualism, provides a promising vision for tomorrow.

It was Easter. Cracked egg shells were in the ashtrays; the floor was carpeted in cellophane grass and foil candy wrappers. The puppy was licking chocolate off Jimmy's face as we sat in a circle in the living room and read and discussed the Easter story. I read a message my Christian guide had given to me for the children. EASTER IS THE TIME TO REJOICE. CHRIST CAME AS A TEACHER—HE CAME TO TEACH PEOPLE TO LOVE ONE ANOTHER. IT IS AS SIMPLE AS THAT—LOVE ONE ANOTHER AND YOU WILL BE FOREVER HAPPY. WHEN CHRIST DIED, MY CHILDREN, HE RETURNED TO THE EARTH. NOW WHEN WE ALL DIE WE CAN RETURN TO THE EARTH AS CHRIST DID. HOWEVER, CHRIST HAD SOME GREATER TALENTS THAN MOST OF US DO. HE COULD RETURN AND WALK AND TALK AMONG YOU. NOW WHEN MOST PEOPLE DIE THEY CANNOT DO THAT. THEY CAN RETURN AND DO THINGS FOR YOU AS YOUR FATHER IS DOING, BUT THEY CAN'T BE SEEN OR HEARD. THE REAL MEANING OF EASTER IS TO SHOW TO ALL PEOPLES THAT LIFE IS EVERLASTING. THAT DEATH DOES NOT END OUR EXISTENCE. CHRIST PROVED THAT BY COMING BACK TO US ON THAT BEAUTIFUL EASTER MORNING MANY MANY YEARS AGO. WE HAVE MANY IMPORTANT SYMBOLS FOR EASTER. THE EGG IS SYMBOLIC OF A NEW LIFE BEGINING. THIS

IS VERY SIMILAR TO WHAT HAPPENS AFTER DEATH. THE LIFE BEGINS AGAIN OR RATHER IT CONTINUES IN A NEW WAY. THE CANDLE IS VERY IMPORTANT BECAUSE IT SYMBOLIZES THE GREAT LIGHT THAT CHRIST SHOWED TO US. THIS REPRESENTS THE LIGHT OF GOD. IF WE LIVE THE LIFE THAT CHRIST TAUGHT US WE WILL BE CLOSER TO THE LIGHT OF GOD. NOW MY CHILDREN, WHEN YOU LIGHT YOUR CANDLES, REMEMBER THIS: BE KIND AND GOOD TO ALL PEOPLE, SHOW THEM YOUR LOVE BY NOT JUDGING THEM BUT BY HELPING THEM AS MUCH AS YOU CAN. ALWAYS BE KIND AND GOOD AND YOU WILL BE CLOSE TO THE LIGHT OF GOD. LIGHT YOUR CANDLES MY CHILDREN AND REMEMBER THEY REPRESENT THE LOVE OF GOD FOR YOU. NOW EASTER IS A BEAUTIFUL TIME OF REJOICING AND HAPPINESS BECAUSE THRU THE DEATH OF CHRIST AND WHEN HE RETURNED WE ALL NOW KNOW THAT DEATH IS NOT AN ENDING BUT A NEW BEGINNING. REJOICE AND CELEBRATE MY CHILDREN AND KNOW THAT THE LIFE AFTER DEATH IS BEAUTIFUL AND HAPPY. YOUR FATHER IS WITH YOU AND THERE ARE MANY OTHERS THAT CELEBRATE WITH YOU. BE JOYOUS AND LOVE ONE ANOTHER.

Mary's sweet little voice broke the quiet of the room after I had finished. "Mom, Georgie's grampa died yesterday and Georgie cries all of the time. He is afraid he is going to die. Golly, if he could only understand what we know, it would make him so happy."

"It would make the world happy too, Mary, if only everyone could understand." Mike answered.

Yes, the world could become happier if it could understand the power and beauty of God as my family does. The awareness of psychic phenomena can give the world the hope for which it so desperately is searching. Psychic study could become the way to the Resurrection of the world. Easter can come again to us through a deeper and broader understanding of a truly living life beyond and Christ's message to each of us can become filled with meaning and vitalize our daily life. A dark society may become enlightened as we intellectually, physically, emotionally, and spiritually understand that the power and love of God is the light of the world. The love of God is in each one. It can be shared by the giving and receiving of love between fellowmen.

LOVE IS THE ANSWER, Mac had written. IT IS THE ONLY THING THAT IS REAL.

The energy of love is infinitely powerful. The energy of God's love created the world. It conceived a cosmos so perfectly balanced by nature that to attempt to comprehend it with our sophisticated and educated minds leaves us overwhelmed.

A woman knows the enormous power of love errupting from her body as the pulsating life of a child is borne from her. Does the child grow enriched only by food, or is it love that makes him laugh and cry, learn and life? A man and woman share their ecstacy as their throbbing bodies become one in the expression of love and communion with each other. It is love that brings us the joy in life. It is the impetus that heals us when we're sick, lights up our eyes, makes us laugh and smile, and assures us that life is worth living. It is the mysterious force that brings light from the darkness, happiness from sorrow, and peace from anxiety.

If only the warm, vibrant energy of love that makes a child's smiling face glow could permeate further into our world. The sparks of life's light that are in each of us through love could fuse and erupt throughout the world like the energy from the splitting of the atom. We, must take the "lid off" the love that we have and let it grow until it crystallizes a new life for the world in peace and harmony.

The challenge is *Now* for mankind and the flame of hope is growing as man searches in many directions to find a greater significance for his being. Although the wars continue, man is delving into himself to discover new ways in which he can become more sensitive to his own needs and those of his fellow man.

Parapsychologists in the Soviet Union and satellite countries have revealed that extensive research and studies have been going on for years in such areas as telepathy, faith healing, auras, brain control, alchemy, eyeless vision and prophecy. They have subjected these and many other occult wonders to true scientific and technological investigation. Their claim is that the discovery of the energy associated with psychic events will be as important if not more important than the discovery of atomic energy. Perhaps an even greater motivation will be the search to unlock the vast storehouse of man's mind, learn to utilize the untapped portion of his brain and open up his unlimited potential.

It appears that the world is witnessing many new discoveries but we are only at the threshold. What mysteries lie behind that door? Although E.S.P. methods were conducted on Apollo 14 to telepathically attempt to transmit signals back to earth, our government has shown little interest in parapsychology. As we become aware of the information the Russians have we feel woefully ignorant. Perhaps our desire to be first will push us like the race for space did and we will enter the contest and begin to scientifically explore the most challenging and exciting of all—the enigmas of man.

The light is around us and available to us all. It can be received if only we ask—if only we believe. For God gives us many great gifts. We have all received them and have witnessed them in others. The differences are only in their magnitude and in our ability to perceive them. Some of us have knowledge, wealth, love, health, beauty, strength, courage, talent or power. There are those who have broken the boundry of consciousness and have opened themselves up to the gifts of the spirit. They have received prophecy, spiritual wisdom, the ability to heal, and communications. God gives them all. He gives in the true essence of giving—freely, spontaneously and selflessly and only through love—a very perfect and beautiful love, which we must all search for and strive to achieve. Those who would judge or try to place a value on these gifts have a difficult task, for the gifts of God can be refused, squandered and misused, but this does not destroy their value—for the gifts of God have been given in love.

How do I really know what I have received is a genuine gift and not just my imagination or a trick of my subconscious mind to help me adjust to death? I have always been a realistic woman who has to cope with whatever might come along. I have dealt with the adjustments and loss that comes with death since childhood. I know death. It has touched me closely many times. I have felt its aches and emptiness. Why now would I be deluded into false reality? How could my mind lie to me so consistantly, so constantly? I am a here and now person and I could no' live a life of delusion and deception.

I began with the belief that all was possible—that God could do all. I chose to be open to the enormous potential available. My mind kept me questioning and searching for answers to the many doubts I had. With ongoing hope I will always be groping and searching, for this way I will grow and learn. We of finite minds have many questions. But, not to question, not to wonder is to close ourselves off from life itself. Questioning is the stimulus that thrusts man forward to seek more knowledge. It becomes the fuel for his intellect. Life is a continual barrage of choices for our free will to handle and a very fine line has to be drawn between the naivete of accepting everything and the suceptibility to want to close it all out. The real doubter shuts the door to the mysteries and magic of life while the gullible person accepts all in a haze of confusion and bewilderment. My experiences have become a constant challenge. I have to humbly admit that I can only believe that they are real because the evidence for their truth is more relevant than the grounds against.

My inadequacies and weaknesses disturb me and make me feel unworthy. Why, oh why did this all happen to me? I question, I wonder. But, while I doubt myself, my Christian guide comes again to counsel me. IT IS RIGHT TO WONDER AND QUESTION MY CHILD BUT NEVER DOUBT THE POWER AND BEAUTY OF GOD. IT IS THRU HIM YOU RECEIVE THE JOYS OF FOREVER HAPPINESS. IT IS THRU HIM YOU RECEIVE THE REAL BEAUTY AND JOY IN THIS WORLD. YES, MY CHILD, BELIEVE THAT HE IS WITH YOU, INSIDE YOU, SURROUNDING YOU THRU THE GLORIES OF THE UNIVERSE AND THE BEAUTY OF OTHER SOULS. MY CHILD BELIEVE.

I do. Thank God!